★

"WE THE PEOPLE WAS CREATED
AS A FORUM FOR THE AMERICAN
PEOPLE TO HEAR THE VOICES
OF SOME OF OUR NATION'S MOST
COMMITTED CITIZENS IN
THIS CRITICAL ELECTION YEAR."

———▶

LOU WEISBACH

Joe Andrew

Hillary Rodham Clir

Chaz Hammelsmith Ebert

Steven Grossman

Peter Max

Marc Pollick

Jonathan Tisch

Andrew Tobias

Kerry Kennedy Cuomo

Alan M. Dershowitz

Deloris Jordan

Joseph Lieberman

Christopher Reeve

Edward Rendell

een Kennedy Townsend

Lou Weisbach

Few families in the history of our country have been more committed to public service from generation to generation than the Kennedys. They remain a great example of how service to your country can further democratic ideals.

We are grateful to the John Fitzgerald Kennedy Library for providing these rare and unique images.

we THE PEOPLE

EDITED BY LOU WEISBACH

DESIGNED AND PRODUCED BY

RARE AIR MEDIA
1711 North Paulina, Suite 311, Chicago, Illinois 60622

Special Thanks
At Rare Air Media:
Elizabeth Fulton, Carol Scatorchio, John Arthurs
Creative: John Vieceli, Steve Polacek
Production: Dennis Carlson, Melinda Fry
Executive Staff: Mark Vancil, Jim Forni, Andy Pipitone

First Edition
Library of Congress Card Number: 00-107442
ISBN 1-892866-30-7
Printed in the United States of America.
10 9 8 7 6 5 4 3 2 1

To my wife Ruth

*My sincere thanks to
all the authors in the book for their
extraordinary contributions.*

———

*A special thanks to
Linda Chester, Jim Forni, Mark Vancil, Elizabeth Fulton,
Steve Polacek, Alana Bruce, Mary Pat Bonner, Mark Fortier,
Rose Weisbach, Irv Kupcinet, Kate Edelman Johnson,
Steve Grossman, and Joe Andrew. All of you have
had a unique impact on this work.*

———

*My profound thanks to
all of you,*

Lou Weisbach

WE THE PEOPLE

★

TABLE OF CONTENTS

FOREWORD
by
LOU WEISBACH

★

s a Democratic activist for many years, and as chair of the Jefferson Trust, the group of the most generous donors to the Democratic Party, I obviously have a strong personal interest in the outcome of the 2000 elections. But as the campaign moves into its final stretch, I feel the need to do more than work behind the scenes, as important as that may be. Like most Americans, I am tired of political platitudes and I am frustrated with politicians who don't listen to the voice of the voters. I think it is vital to let the American people hear directly from some of our nation's most committed citizens and that is why I decided to create WE THE PEOPLE.

In a deeply personal way, the contributors to this book tell why they are inspired and energized by the ideals of the Democratic Party. These leaders from the worlds of politics, community service, business, law and entertainment explain why the Democratic Party is the vehicle through which their ideas and passions are cultivated, and the institution on which they depend to realize their social, economic and political values. Together, they clearly articulate the importance of the Democratic Party in their lives, in the history of America and in the everyday lives of all Americans. Above all, they tell why they believe it is crucial to elect Al Gore and Joe Lieberman in November, and to take back control of the House and the Senate.

In putting together this book, I also wanted to draw attention to the critical issues that are of pressing concern to me, such as gun control, health care and human rights. I wanted to shine a spotlight on the very real differences between the Democrats and Republicans on education, Social Security and Medicare, the Supreme Court, the environment, a woman's right to choose and many other issues. As Kerry Kennedy Cuomo writes in her essay: "It's too easy to forget, in the voting booth, that the real results of a Republican victory would mean a White House-led effort to abolish the U.S. Department of Education, a repeal of the minimum wage laws, a phase-out of the Social Security system, a repeal of the 'motor-voter' law, an adoption of 'American English' as the official language of the nation and an end to all forms of U.S. participation in the United Nations. It sounds extreme, but it comes directly from the Republican platform."

This book celebrates America's remarkable achievements during the Clinton-Gore administration: the strongest economy in history; a vast increase in wealth; the highest rate of home ownership ever; rising incomes at every level; budget surpluses instead of deficits; a world at peace; and the lowest unemployment, welfare and crime rates in a generation. Many of us, including myself and my family, have been blessed by financial prosperity that our parents and grandparents hardly could have imagined.

My wife, Ruth, has a particular passion and that is helping less fortunate people who have not yet benefited from the nation's economic good times. She believes it is crucial that we use our success to lift up the working families of America. We need to raise the minimum wage. We need to implement the targeted and fiscally responsible tax cuts proposed by Al Gore to help families struggling to pay for education, child care, health insurance and prescription drugs, rather than the huge giveaway to the wealthy that the Republicans are proposing.

I do these things because they give me joy, because my faith urges me to do them and because I am a Democrat. I want to help make my party's most basic principles a reality. As Andy Tobias, treasurer of the Democratic National Committee, says in his essay, those principles are opportunity for all, special privilege for none and a community that encourages the best in all of us. Or as Christopher Reeve put it in his moving speech at the 1996 Democratic national convention, "America does not let its needy citizens fend for themselves. America is stronger when all of us take care of all of us." Together with other Democrats, we embrace a party that doesn't just pay lip service to the magnificent diversity of America, but has a long history of embracing that diversity.

I believe that a decisive choice lies before us in November that will affect the direction our country takes for many years to come. When you use your car transmission, you choose D to go forward or R to go backward. To control the transmission of the government, you have to choose D for Democrat to go forward. If you choose R for Republican, our government will go backward and we will have wasted the progress we've made in the last eight years.

In the 21st century, new challenges, new technologies, and a new economy are changing the way that Americans think about politics. But the bedrock principles of the Democrats still offer the best hope for creating a future with both prosperity and purpose. As Franklin D. Roosevelt taught us, America is a better and more secure country when we give a helping hand to those who have been left behind. As Harry Truman famously put it, "The buck stops here." And as John F. Kennedy said in his acceptance speech before the 1960 Democratic national convention in Los Angeles, "I think the American people expect more from us than cries of indignation and attack. ... We are not here to curse the darkness, but to light the candle that can guide us through that darkness to a safe and sane future." Along with the other contributors to WE THE PEOPLE, I believe with all my mind and heart that the Democrats are the ones who can get us there.

CHAPTER ONE

★

JOE
ANDREW

WHY AM I A DEMOCRAT?

Northern Indiana is flat. Fields of wheat, corn and soybeans stretch out to the horizon, undulating in the breeze like a great green ocean. The old prairie between Detroit and Indianapolis was leveled by the glaciers, leaving great expanses without a hill, a dell or a canyon. When an individual stands on that plain, there is no mountain to humble you, no hilly forest to block your view. You can see forever and you appear as the most important thing on the landscape.

The flatlands breed cows and confidence — and an undeserved certainty that you are right, a libertarian worship of the individual and an anti-historical perspective. Everything is new because there is so little to remind you of yesterday. Everything is you because there is so little else around. This is where I was born. This is where I grew up.

I am proud to be elected as the National Chair of the Democratic Party, but how I got to this position, and how I became a Democrat, is a mystery to most people who don't know me well. For, you see, I am not a genetic Democratic, or a geographic Democrat, or a generational Democrat, or a gender Democrat, or a got-to-get-mine Democrat. I've been a Democrat surrounded by Republicans from my earliest memories. I'm a Democrat for the simple reason that by the time I was 8 years old, it was obvious to me that on every issue that counts, Democrats were probably right and Republicans were usually wrong. It's just that Republicans always seemed so certain that they were right and Democrats were certain only that the world was complex.

I was born into a Lutheran family of not very politically active Republicans who had every reason to be Democrats. My father had grown up in poverty and had brought his entire family into the middle class with hard work, luck and help from the GI Bill. I grew up in a very conservative part of the flatlands of Northern Indiana that even voted for Goldwater when Johnson won Indiana in 1964, the only time since FDR that a Democrat won Indiana. My grandparents, save one, were Republicans. My aunts and uncles and cousins and neighbors were certain, conservative, judgmental Republicans — or worse, they simply weren't involved.

I am part of a generation that lacks definition — too young to really be a part of the baby boomers, too old to be part of Generation X. I was born in 1960, too late to participate in the civil rights marches, the love-ins, the protests against the Vietnam War. On the farm I grew up in near the little town of Poe, Indiana, all of the noise and commotion was something we saw on TV, but did not participate in. We were the spectator generation. Watching. Entertained. Troubled. Looking for a reason to change channels. We knew what was on TV was important, but it seemed irrelevant to getting the hay bailed, the corn planted, the animals watered and fed every day. Desegregation and busing enlarged our world, but for most of my generation our political consciousness began with Watergate and ended with Ronald Reagan. Government was either corrupt or hapless. Politics was either crass or pointless. And it was all on TV — the only certain perspective was the angle the camera was pointed.

My older cousin was the leader in the Young Republicans and led our county's Youth for Nixon Committee and I remember him teaching my brothers and sisters to taunt me because I wrote to Bobby Kennedy's campaign to get a campaign button. Bobby Kennedy was in Indiana the night that Martin Luther King was killed and while he gave one of the most eloquent speeches of the 20th century that night, the local newspaper editorialized against him from the front page of the paper. In the midst of the poetry and the passion, I pouted because I had never received my button.

As I grew older, the women in my family were becoming more liberal and my black friends were becoming more active, but I was a white, Anglo-Saxon, heterosexual middle class male who aspired to go to an Ivy league school and make lots of money. I was interested in sports cars and bell bottoms, not civil rights and getting out of Vietnam. But I announced to everyone that I was a Democrat, not as an act of rebellion, or guilt or contrition, but of logic. Civil rights was the right thing. Getting out of Vietnam was the right thing. Progressive taxation was the right thing. Investing in education was the right thing. Making health care more accessible was the right thing. Protecting social security was the right thing.

It was just so clear to me, so logical. Everyone else around me just didn't get it. They were genetic Republicans. Geographic Republicans. They were certain that they were right and were willing to assert their positions, from my perspective, without qualms, consideration or caveats. They stood tall on the earth — rock solid, confident conservatives — while I tried to work out each problem in my mind, weighing the pros and cons, coming to the logical conclusion.

The day Bobby Kennedy was killed, school was let out early because all the town's leading citizens expected riots that never came to Northern Indiana, so I was home when the mail came. There was a small manila-colored package for me in the stack of letters. It was a Bobby Kennedy campaign button.

I worked on my first Democratic campaign four years later when I was 12, handing out literature for a congressional candidate that both of my parents voted against. I volunteered for the county Democrat Party when I was 14; my mother dropping me off only because I threatened to hitchhike if she didn't drive me there. All through high school I talked and talked and talked. Trying to convince, to cajole, to compel others to see the logic of our cause.

I went on to Yale and then law school where I met thousands of Democrats, but I remember how people in high school made fun of my Democratic activism — including Democrats. Of course the Republicans thought I was simply crazy, but the Democrats weren't so keen on me. Black kids didn't trust me because I was white. Hispanic kids made fun of my Spanish. Gay kids didn't trust me because I had a girlfriend. Poor kids resented that I had my own car. Older people thought I was too young. Young people thought I wasn't hip. Catholic friends thought I didn't understand. Union kids resented my white collar. Smart kids thought I was wasting my time.

By choice, I made myself different simply because I believed I was right, my party was right, and Republicans were wrong.

But a funny thing happened on my way to minority status — I started convincing people to come along with me. My grandmother was my first convert when one day she suddenly announced to me that she had been lying to my grandfather for 30 years and secretly voting for Democrats. She became active and when I showed off my Bobby Kennedy button she showed me a photograph of her that was taken on the day FDR died.

On the day that FDR died my grandmother was a single mother working as a seamstress making 23 cents an hour. She was a supervisor, so she made 3 cents more an hour than anyone else on the line. Later she became a bookkeeper. As a single woman in the last years of the war, no one would rent her an apartment or a house, so she was forced to live in the old Harrison Hotel in Fort Wayne, Indiana, with her two sons who were 9 and 11. After a week or two of living in the hotel, the management gave her the classic Sophie's choice — two boys were just too much, she could stay only with one. So she sent her younger son, my father, off to live on a farm with her sister and kept her older son with her.

On the day FDR died, my grandmother, the seamstress, went out and bought every yard of black fabric she could find in that small prairie town. She brought the bolts of cloth back to the hotel and began draping the balconies and the balustrades. People came out to help her and, when they were finished, the night clerk took a picture of them standing in the hotel lobby. My grandmother looking tired and an African-American woman in a waitress uniform, her apron wrinkled into a work of black and white art. The janitor with a mop in his hand and a pack of Lucky Strikes rolled up in his sleeve. A traveling salesman with his Fedora cocked back on his head, a silver flask peeking out from his breast pocket. A woman in a full-length mink coat.

They all came out to help my grandmother, she explained to me, not because of any program or policy initiated by FDR, although they were all so important, but because he stood up for all of them. They stood together, teary-eyed in that photograph, not because of rural electrification, or the FEC or the FDA or beginnings of the struggles for civil rights and social security. They cried not because FDR conquered the Great Depression, gave us the New Deal and saved the world from totalitarian dictatorship. They cried, my grandmother explained, rolling my Bobby Kennedy button around in her gnarled, age-spotted hands, because FDR stood up for them. The patrician millionaire stood up for my grandmother making 23 cents an hour. A man who could not stand up himself because he had polio, he was 40, stood up for all Americans, all the time.

That is why they were Democrats and in the end, why I am a Democrat. Not because of programs and policies, but because of perspective and philosophy. Not because of great liberal icons such as FDR or Bobby Kennedy, nor great centrist icons such as Bill Clinton and Al Gore. Not because of labels, but because of logic. Not because of my grandmother's treasured photograph or my rusty campaign button, but because of the helping hand they symbolize.

We stand up for people who don't stand so tall themselves. We stand up for people lost in the hills and canyons of real life. We stand up for the people who need someone else to stand, not to stand alone. We stand for people not so certain that they are right and others are wrong. We stand up for people who see shades of many colors where others see only black and white.

Decades later, I am a father myself now and my children are surrounded by Democrats. Indiana went on, and in the late '80s began electing hundreds of Democratic officeholders. President Clinton and Vice-President Gore broadened our Party, bringing more people into the Democratic Party than any time in a generation. The participants of the '60s, the spectators of the '70s, the skeptics of the '80s, and the well-wired of the '90s, all have joined our Party.

As the National Chair of the oldest political party in the world, with my campaign button and tattered photograph, let me say one thing: Welcome. Welcome to the Democratic Party. You're home now.

JOE ANDREW

Joseph J. Andrew is the National Chair of the Democratic National Committee. Elected in March 1999, Andrew has proven to be a skilled political strategist through integrating high-tech ideas of new politics with traditional grassroots organizing. As a CEO, lawyer, published author, technology expert, father and Democrat activist, Andrew has led a full life.

After his election as DNC National Chair, Andrew formulated a plan designed to build on the tremendous achievements of his predecessors. His creation of the Democratic Mayors Campaign Committee sparked victories across the ballot in the 1999 municipal elections, as Democrats won all five of the targeted mayoral races. Andrew guided the DNC out of debt and, in partnership with General Chair Ed Rendell, out-raised the Republican National Committee for the first time in a generation. And under Andrew's management, the DNC ended the first quarter of 2000 with more cash on hand than at anytime in its 152-year history. By implementing 21st century technology and grassroots mobilization efforts, Andrew steadily has equipped the DNC with the necessary resources to be effective in races up and down the ballot.

A life-long Democrat, Joe Andrew served as the Chair of the Indiana Democratic Party from 1995-1999. In both 1996 and 1998, Andrew led the Party to unprecedented state victories. Under his leadership, the Indiana Democratic Party raised more money per capita than any Democratic state party in the nation, created the first statewide Inclusion Committee and oversaw the most diverse delegations to both the State and National Conventions in the state's history. As a member of the team led by Senator Evan Bayh and

Governor Frank O'Bannon, Andrew helped Indiana elect more Democratic officeholders with fewer self-identified Democratic voters than any other state in America.

Andrew, 40, grew up on a farm in Allen County, Indiana. He graduated magna cum laude from Yale University and The Yale Law School, where he was a Glen Peters Legal Scholar. Andrew clerked on the Seventh Circuit Court of Appeals and has practiced intellectual property and corporate law for 15 years.

Andrew is the author of a spy novel, "The Disciples," published by Simon and Schuster. He is the founder of a bio-technology and internet business development firm and a corporate consumer insight analyst in a prominent advertising group. He has served on numerous non-profit boards, including those as diverse as legal services for the indigent and historic preservation.

Joe Andrew is married to Anne Slaughter Andrew, an attorney, National Board Member of the Women's Leadership Forum and Democratic activist. They have two young children and now reside in a Washington, DC suburb.

CHAPTER TWO

HILLARY
RODHAM CLINTON

MAKING WOMENS' VOICES VITAL IN THE POLITICAL WORLD

First Lady Hillary Rodham Clinton has long championed women's issues, including an expanded role for women in civic life and politics. She believes that grass-roots participation is the cornerstone of democracy and that social and political action are keys to uplifting citizens — especially women — whose voices too often go unheard in the corridors of power. This article is excerpted from a speech she delivered to the Senior Executive Women's Forum in Chicago, Illinois, October 26, 1999.

embers of the National American Women's Suffrage Association gathered on February 14, 1920 at the Congress Hotel in Chicago for their last convention. They knew that the 19th amendment would soon be ratified. So the meeting began with a celebration as they sang "The Battle Hymn of the Republic" and "There will be a Hot Time in the Old Town Tonight."

Imagine what those women, those pioneers, would think if they were here today and knew that women held very high positions in corporations, as general counsels, vice-presidents and presidents; that they held office, that they were candidates for office; that they had taken the work and the sacrifice of those who came before and pushed it even further, and by doing so made it possible for women to dream even bigger dreams. . . .

Will we be role models for the women and girls who follow us? I believe we can, but we have to be very conscious about the lessons we are teaching and the gifts we are giving. It requires us to think a little differently, perhaps, than our foremothers ever could have imagined and to realize that politics is part of how we do anything in a democracy. Politics with a small "p" matters in all of our lives because as citizens of this democracy each of us has an obligation to participate. Jane Addams once said, "Politics is … housekeeping on a grand scale." What she showed . . . is that civic involvement is really the lifeblood of democracy. It is how we make decisions, how we move closer to our ideals as Americans.

The delegates who gathered at the Congress Hotel in 1920 adopted resolutions on issues ranging from the minimum wage to education, to equal opportunity for women in politics and business. But it was up to the women who came after, and particularly the women of the last decade, to bring those issues to the top of the political agenda. We know that there is a so-called "gender gap" in elections. But many issues debated daily in the media and in Congress — whether health care or education or domestic violence or child care — are no longer just women's issues. They are issues for the entire body politic. When children don't have a safe place to go after school, when women don't earn equal pay for equal work, those issues affect families and communities.

I recall during the 1996 election when some political commentators said that the focus on issues like child care was leading to a "feminization of politics." I think they meant it as an insult. But I prefer to think of it as the *humanization* of politics. What we are talking about is how people actually live their lives, and how we can ensure that politics works.

When someone asks, "Does it matter whether women are involved in politics?," I think of the last 6½ years. It certainly has mattered to women and to families that we have record unemployment, record surpluses, the strongest economy in a generation and more women-owned businesses than ever before.

It matters that crime is down and that health insurance is being extended to children; that the Family and Medical Leave Act is ensuring that parents won't have to choose between the job they need and the child they love.

But at this time of unprecedented prosperity and opportunity, we — men and women — face a fundamental choice: Are we satisfied that the progress we have made is good enough? Are we ready to retreat into our own private sphere and say, "I'm fine, my family's fine, my business is fine; I don't have to worry about anyone else?" Or do we take advantage of this moment to confront the challenges that we all still face?

Right now decisions are being made at the national, state and local level that will determine the quality of our lives into the next century. Right now, almost two-thirds of women with small children are in the labor force. What happens in Washington, and in capitals across the country, will determine whether or not millions of low-income families are eligible for child care subsidies and whether parents will have a safe place for their children after school.

Never before has a good education been more of a passport to prosperity — or a bad education more of a life-sentence. What will happen to the 5,000 school buildings across America that need to be repaired or replaced? What will happen to the nearly 1.7 million school children who are now in smaller classes because we passed the initiative to put 100,000 more teachers in the classroom?

Right now, decisions are being made that will determine whether women will finally receive equal pay for equal work. One of my staff members showed me a cartoon that her mother had sent her, which she stuck up on the refrigerator at home. It showed six people sitting around a conference room table — all in suits, all wearing glasses, all men. And one of them announces, "Gentlemen, we must cut our expenses in half, so I'm replacing each of you with a woman."

… Clearly, things are not that bad. The gap between women's and men's wages has narrowed since 1963, when the Equal Pay Act was passed. But women still bring home only about 75 cents for every man's dollar, and we now have some very sophisticated studies about the persistence of wage discrimination at the highest levels of our academic and business worlds. And we know that a 25-cent difference isn't much comfort when you have to pay expenses that keep a family going.

Right now, decisions are being made that will determine whether we pass, and the President signs, a Patient's Bill of Rights for every American; whether we save and strengthen Medicare and Social Security for future generations. Those are two programs that are especially important to women. Nearly a quarter of all elderly women rely on Social Security as their sole source of income. And because women live longer than men do, they have more chronic health problems, relatively smaller pensions, and therefore depend on Medicare even more.

... Politics is about organizing and raising [our] voices here at home and around the world.

I've been privileged to represent our country in many different settings and I have seen first-hand the struggles that women face around the globe. It often puts into stark perspective our own situation. I've been in villages in Africa and small huts in Asia and health clinics in Latin America, and I've listened to countless women talk about their lives. I think it's a good reminder to think about what it's like for the majority of women living in other parts of the world who often put in very long hours — getting up before the sun to gather firewood, to milk a goat, or even, as I saw in Mongolia, a horse; to prepare the food that often takes hours; to do the planting and the harvesting; to go to the market; to be employed by or run the small businesses that are the backbones of most developing countries' economies — and who still, with all of their effort, often find themselves ignored, marginalized within their families and their communities.

We started an initiative called Vital Voices and we have taken that initiative throughout the world so that we could give a platform to women's voices, and by doing so, try to help women become political. We started in Austria with women from the former Soviet Union. And we listened to women who once held positions and now find themselves unemployed because the jobs are scarcer, and men often receive them.

We moved on to Latin America where we had a hemispheric conference in Uruguay, where woman after woman talked about what it meant to no longer be living under totalitarian military dictatorships. Every country in our hemisphere, save one, is now a democracy. Many of those women had stood on the front lines as they saw loved ones disappear, as they saw democracy return after very difficult battles, and they were determined to take their rightful place in every sector of society. I attended a joint meeting of all the women in the legislature in Uruguay — of every political stripe, from the far right to the far left — who had banded together to make sure women's voices were heard.

In Belfast, Northern Ireland, we convened a Vital Voices conference and brought together women from the north who had never sat down and talked with one another — women from different traditions who found they had more in common and could make common cause in the political system. Women have been elected to the assembly in Northern Ireland, and we are all hopeful that the peace process takes hold and moves forward. But on the ground, in the small "p" political arena, women are knitting communities together, crossing sectarian lines, creating small businesses, building play-grounds in areas where children have never felt safe to play outdoors.

And then I was in Iceland, where women from Russia and the Baltics came together with women from Scandinavia and America to talk about democracy. There are so many challenges facing the women of Russia. Yet they were there, bravely looking for ways to help themselves and their communities become political participants in a very difficult environment. Women from other parts of the world also came to speak. Rasha, from Kuwait, spoke about how after years of struggle, the Emir had said that women would be permitted to vote, but the Parliament has yet to act on that decree. The parliamentary leaders keep saying, "What is the urgency?" And Rasha said she had been stunned by the question. These women had stood shoulder to shoulder during the Iraqi invasion. They had undertaken very difficult, and sometimes even dangerous, missions and they are still being told to wait.

A woman from Belarus — Vera, a lawyer who stands up for human rights in a country that is reverting to communism and totalitarian authoritarianism — spoke movingly about what it's like to be a lawyer who speaks for human rights when your colleagues disappear, when you're disbarred, when newspapers are shut down.

These examples remind us that we have many blessings, not just in comparison to the women who met at the Congress Hotel, or the women who helped Jane Addams with projects she undertook at Hull House, or the women at Seneca Falls in 1848 who published their Declaration of Sentiments on behalf of women. We are so blessed in comparison to women in many parts of the world right now.

Any blessing also carries an obligation. What will we do to make sure our voices are heard? We have the blessings we enjoy today not because some benevolent ruler gave them to us, but because we worked for them, we advocated for them, we struggled for them, and, yes we voted for them.

We live in an extraordinary moment in history as we end this 20th century. We can decide to honor the past and imagine and build a better future, or we can allow the complacency that often sets in when times are good to dull our senses and close our eyes to the work that is yet to be done. If we want to honor the past, then we have to be part of imagining and making that future.

We've seen an increasing reluctance of people to vote. One of my favorite posters from 1996 was of a woman with a piece of tape covering her mouth. And under it, it said: "Most politicians think women should be seen and not heard. In the last election, 54 million women agreed with them."

So the bottom line, the most fundamental obligation, is to vote. It's surprising how many people of affluence and standing tell me that they have given up on the political process; they don't think there is any difference; they don't vote because they don't think it matters. And I always ask them whether it mattered that we turned the economy around, that it was a hard-fought legislative battle. I ask them whether they think it matters that we did finally pass a Family and Medical Leave Act, that now 20 million Americans have taken advantage of. I ask them whether they think it matters that finally, against the extraordinary opposition of the NRA, the Brady Bill was passed and now more than 400,000 people have been turned away from their efforts to buy a weapon.

I think those things do matter. I think, as we look across the landscape of America today, we can see how it matters that our prosperity is lifting so many people — their incomes, their fortunes, their futures are rising.

Eleanor Roosevelt, one of my favorite predecessors, wrote a very influential essay back in the 1920s about women in politics. She said that women had to be much better prepared than men, that women had to be ready to be questioned and criticized, that women had to grow skin as thick as a rhinoceros. But she urged women to take all of the necessary steps to be politically active. She understood, as she often said, that you must do the thing you think you cannot do. And one of my favorite Eleanor Roosevelt sayings is, "Women are like teabags, they don't know how strong they are until they get into hot water."

... I am often asked, when will a woman be president? Eleanor Roosevelt was asked and she said by the 1970s. In the 1970s, Rosalynn Carter was asked and she said by the year 2000. So to play it safe, I'll say in the 21st century. Part of the reason it's so difficult is because of the way we finance campaigns. I hope that women's voices will be heard more loudly in the effort to change the campaign finance rules, because they are undermining our democracy and undermining the voices of many citizens.

Voting, raising your voice, supporting candidates, advocating for change — they are all ways that each of us can participate. And then there is the next step — one that more and more women are taking — to become candidates, and to serve in public life.

For those who do hold office, it's a real challenge to keep focused on the issues that matter. In our system, you are elected to Congress, or governor, or senator, or to the state legislature. And many who are elected have to start immediately campaigning for office again, and that means raising the money necessary to fund those campaigns.

So there are many people – men and women — who are resigning or failing to run because they don't think the process works.

There is no reason why women cannot be at the forefront of reforming the political process and completing the unfinished business of the 20th century — to continue our economic progress and make sure it reaches every single American; to continue reforming our public education system and ensure that every child has a chance to learn and has access to the information age technology that he or she will require; to make it possible for us to once again put patients and doctors in the center of the health care system; to ensure that we do what is necessary to keep guns out of the hands of children and criminals; to protect our environment. . .

We will also face new challenges . . . ensuring that we finally have a health care system that provides quality, affordable health care to every American; looking for ways to marry the environment and the economy so that we don't pit one against the other; ensuring that the digital divide is just a phrase and not a fact that further widens the wealth gap in our country; working on the unfinished business of making this one America where all people are respected and have a chance to participate fully; continuing to lead around the world and making clear that America is the strongest force for peace and prosperity and stability, and that means looking for ways to end the spread of nuclear weapons, and dealing with threats like global warming and proliferation of chemical and biological weapons, and ensuring that we are up to speed on our public health agenda to limit the spread of epidemics or other challenges. There is much much work to be done.

I was recently at a conference about the future of politics and I was there with a very distinguished British scholar who studies political developments around the world. And he said, the most important change in the 20th century has been the role of women. American women have broken new ground, have navigated uncharted waters. And he turned to me and said: "Will American women keep doing so, or will they be satisfied just to try to balance the demands of their own lives?" It was a good question. And the answer is that we will continue to do what we can to use politics to advance the common good. And by doing so, we will continue to demonstrate the leadership that women have shown in the past and that we have tried to live up to.

———

HILLARY RODHAM CLINTON

When Hillary Rodham Clinton spoke at her commencement at Wellesley College in 1969, she talked about politics as "the art of making what appears to be impossible,

possible." More than 30 years later, she remains faithful to that vision. From working to improve the conditions of children and families in the United States to championing democracy and human rights around the world, she has become one of our nation's most eloquent and influential voices for social justice and social progress.

Hillary Clinton was born in Chicago, Illinois in 1947 and raised in nearby Park Ridge where she attended local public schools. After graduating from Wellesley, she attended Yale Law School and met her future husband, Bill Clinton, a fellow student. While at law school, she volunteered her time working on foster care and abuse cases and providing legal services to the poor. Her experience there would set the stage for a lifelong commitment to advocacy and a wide range of children and family issues.

For more than three decades, Hillary Clinton has fought for better health care, expanded educational opportunities, improvements in child care and economic security for all Americans, especially women. As first lady of the United States, she has left an indelible imprint on policies affecting foster care and adoption, breast cancer treatment and detection, expansions of Medicare funding, child care and after-school care, health insurance for poor children and families, tax deductions for college tuition, legal services for the poor, the arts and humanities and many other issues. Her philosophy and beliefs are outlined in a book she wrote in 1995 entitled "It Takes a Village and Other Lessons Children Teach Us."

Hillary Clinton also has been a champion of democracy and human rights, especially for girls and women in the developing world. She has worked tirelessly to promote education, microfinance and family planning as essential tools for women to fulfill their potential in life. In her extensive travels, she has been a leading voice for the democratic principles of freedom, equality and social justice. She has encouraged women to become involved in the political process through her Vital Voices Initiative, which brings women from around the world together to share ideas about how to be effective agents of political change.

Hillary Clinton is the proud mother of daughter Chelsea and currently is running for the United States Senate as the Democratic candidate from New York.

First Lady Hillary Rodham Clinton long has championed women's issues, including an expanded role for women in civic life and politics. She believes that grass-roots participation is the cornerstone of democracy and that social and political action are keys to uplifting citizens – especially women — whose voices too often go unheard in the corridors of power. This article is excerpted from a speech she delivered to the Senior Executive Women's Forum in Chicago, Illinois, October 26, 1999.

CHAPTER THREE

★

KERRY
KENNEDY CUOMO

THE MANY BRIDGES
YET TO CROSS

When Democrats from every corner of America gathered in Los Angeles this summer to nominate Al Gore to become the 43rd President of the United States, there was a fact lost on few that many inside the Staples Center, where the convention was held, were not alive in 1960, 40 years ago, the last time that Los Angeles provided the backdrop to our party's quadrennial gathering. I am one of those Democrats who was barely alive, born just eight months before, and did not have the privilege to witness my uncle, John F. Kennedy, accepting our party's nomination.

This year, in Los Angeles, the scene was ripe with nostalgia, both for my family and for Democrats everywhere. To ready myself for the event that was both a look back in our memory and a glimpse into our future, I pulled out the scrapbooks from Memorial Coliseum on the night of July 15, 1960, the evening that the Kennedy/Johnson ticket was introduced to the nation. What I found was a speech by my uncle that was as appropriate for our time as it was for his.

Standing atop the sweltering podium, about half way through the speech, surrounded by the party faithful, he said this:

"I think the American people expect more from us than cries of indignation and attack. The times are too grave, the challenge too urgent and the stakes too high – to permit the customary passions of political debate. We are not here to curse the darkness, but to light the candle that can guide us through that darkness to a safe and sane future. As Winston Churchill said on taking office some 20 years ago: if we open a quarrel between the present and the past, we shall be in danger of losing the future."

Even though he could look back at his time in military service, even though he could look back at his time in the House of Representatives or the U.S. Senate, he decided instead to look forward during his brief speech. "Today our concern must be with that future. For the world is changing. The old era is ending. The old ways will not do."

John Kennedy knew that America's interests overseas bore directly on our direction at home. In many ways, he was prescient. "Abroad, the balance of power is shifting. There are new and more terrible weapons – new and uncertain nations – new pressures of population and deprivation. One-third of the world, it has been said, may be free – but one-third is the victim of cruel repression – and the other one-third is rocked by the pangs of poverty, hunger and envy. More energy is released by the awakening of these new nations than by the fission of the atom itself."

The echo of those words seem to have bounced through the years, reverberating from decade to decade. As we read them, we take pride in the fact that many of his hopes and aspirations have been adopted by both well-intentioned Democrats and well-intentioned Republicans alike. We take pride that our schools have been integrated. We take pride that our people have been put back to work at a rate equaling the levels while he was in office. We take pride that we won the Cold War and watched as Communist and totalitarian dictatorships fell, year after year, and that today only a few remain. We take pride that medical advances have rid us of what, back then, seemed incurable diseases.

We take pride that America, which then was slipping into a self-satisfied economic state, soon to fall behind Asia and Europe which had been rebuilt with our help after World War II, now leads the world in practically every category of economic efficiency.

But the echo of his words, when they take a different bounce, smack us with the realization that today, as in 1960, we still face many of the persistent problems that seem to cut down party lines. Remember what he said: "Today our concern must be with that future. For the world is changing. The old era is ending. The old ways will not do."

Let there be a true voice, heard loud and clear this summer and fall, that his job is not finished, and nor is the job for Democrats everywhere. Bill Clinton said in 1996 that he and Al Gore wanted to "build a bridge to the 21st Century." In that effort, they succeeded. We are here. We are whole. We are a nation again.

But that optimism cannot breed complacency. And that optimism cannot allow us to lessen our guard against forces that would undo all the accomplishments for which we take pride. There are too many bridges yet to cross, and we have only just begun.

For my part, as a human rights activist and somewhat of an observer of how Washington ebbs and flows, I want to remind us all of how much work still is unfinished, of how many social problems persist, even on our watch. We must trumpet our achievements, true enough, but we must also sing the blues of jobs undone and of great efforts torn asunder by relentless hatreds and persistent evil that still threatens to pull our nation apart.

As I wrote this, I scanned the newspapers and went to the sports pages. With the exception of John Rocker, news from the world of sport is relatively free from violence and hate.

Within those pages, there is great joy to be savored.

Venus Williams, a 20-year-old African-American woman, wins Wimbledon, the first African American woman since Althea Gibson in 1958 to do so.

Tiger Woods, of Asian-American and African-American descent, so dominates the game of golf that few can imagine another competitor for years to come who will challenge his hegemony. He wins tournaments at golf courses where, not too long ago, there would have been unwritten rules preventing him from even teeing off.

Pedro Martinez, an immigrant from the Dominican Republic, routinely sends baseball's mightiest sluggers back to their dugouts, barely aware of the ball's nuance that rendered their bats useless. He is the toast of the City of Boston, a town that rarely has been so welcoming of outsiders.

America's World Cup champion women's soccer team, a phrase of words never before strung, prepares to go to Sydney to defend their dominance of what traditionally has been a foreign-dominated and male-dominated sport. In Los Angeles in 1998, they beat the best female soccer players on the planet and are expected to be similarly successful in Australia.

If only life could begin and end with the sports pages.

The front section of the newspaper arrived on our doorstep, too, and I can't help absorbing it with as much trepidation as the sports pages provided celebration.

Reading the front page must give us pause, because for all the things that are right with America, there are too many things that are still not right with America. And there are even more things that are still not right with the world, for which America must take some responsibility (and I would argue that if we are to re-embrace the words of my uncle, my father, Franklin Roosevelt, Martin Luther King and Bill Clinton, we must accept even more responsibility than we previously have been willing to take).

Next to the columns that show a surging economy, record employment and new strides in technological advancement, there are these, from that day's:

Kokomo, Mississippi. Raynard Johnson, a 17-year old African American is found last month hanging from the branch of a pecan tree on his front lawn. The authorities have said it was a suicide, but there are too many questions to dismiss the possibility that Raynard was lynched. Lynched? In America? In the year 2000? That's just the most unthinkable event of what we know is a persistent racial conflict still raging across our nation. We have to ask ourselves, as we read of such reports, whose Administration will take a more serious approach toward ending such atrocities? George W. Bush or Al Gore? A man who has been handed one elective office and seeks another? Or a man who has spent an entire career in public service in battle against these plagues?

Let's read on, but it only gets worse.

Grant Town, West Virginia. Two teenagers beat a gay man to death then run over his body several times to make it appear to be a hit-and-run accident. The man, Arthur Warren, a Baptist church usher, had complained in the past about harassment in his town, but the complaints were not heard by the authorities. Again, an isolated incident, or a plague upon our land?

A brief look back at the archives.

Have the names Matthew Shepherd or James Byrd Jr. escaped our memory? They should not. They should be seared in our brains. Shepherd, a gay man, was beaten and left for dead in Wyoming. Byrd, a black man, was chained to a back of a pickup truck by three white men and dragged over a logging road leaving a three-mile trail of his body parts. We have to ask ourselves, as we read of such reports, whose Administration will take a more serious approach toward ending such atrocities that still plague our country. George W. Bush or Al Gore?

Last item from the home front.

In Texas last month, Gary Graham was put to death in Texas for a murder he said he did not commit. I didn't review all the evidence and I don't know whether or not to believe him. But I know that the Supreme Court did review his case, and by a 5-4 margin, they refused his final round of appeals. Is there anything that makes you uneasy about a 5-4 decision of any sort? It had to have been a close call and we're talking about the state taking a man's life. Is a close call acceptable on such terms? The next president will have the opportunity to appoint as many as three new justices to the Supreme Court. Who do you want vetting the names of the people who will decide the fate of capital punishment in this country – to say nothing of a woman's right to choose, or staples of our judicial system such as the Miranda warning? A man who has helped pick Justices Ginsburg and Breyer for the highest court in the land? Or a man who is content to let his state's Clemency Board rule on the fate of a man's life via the fax machine?

A few more items from today's paper, from overseas.

Despite the many positive movements toward peace in my ancestral homeland, Ireland, for which we owe so much to President Clinton and Vice-President Gore, the Orange Order persists in its efforts to march, recalling their past military triumphs, through Catholic neighborhoods in the North. Friends there tell me it threatens to plunge the island into another interminable period of instability. Again, let's ask, on Day One of the term of the 43rd President of the United States, who will know better how to allay the oncoming storm of hostility in Belfast? The Vice-President, who has monitored every move of the peace process during the last eight years? Or the Governor of Texas who, before being elected to that office, owned a baseball team?

Next item.

Prime Minister Ehud Barak and PLO Chairman Yasir Arafat were to arrive in the U.S. shortly to sequester themselves at Camp David until they can resolve the final differences with keeping a lasting peace from taking hold in the Middle East. They ultimately may succeed, or they may fail, but their embattled part of the world is far from finally resolving the thousands of years of hostility that divide the peoples on that small sliver of land. And what of Syria? And growing religious tensions in Egypt? And the challenges facing King Abdullah of Jordan? Again, on whom can we rely to take up the reigns of the significant progress that has been made over the last eight years? The man who was a critical part of every move that was made, who has participated in every face-to-face meeting with the warring leaders in the Oval Office? Or a man who would be hard pressed, if asked, to conjure their names?

Let's move to Russia.

In Moscow, President Putin delivers his first state of the nation address. During the 50-minute address, he says that in the 10 years since overthrowing Soviet Rule, Russians have built "only the carcass" of civil society, and pledges to get to work dutifully to instill the heart and flesh of such a society within that carcass. You want to give him the benefit of the doubt, but you know that one of the easiest – and, in the long run, foolhardy – tools to deploy would be to centralize power, clamp down on the freedom of the press and trample the human and civil rights that are still just beginning to take hold. It wouldn't be too much of a risk if it weren't for the barely countable stockpile of weapons of mass destruction that sit loosely guarded in naval bases and missile silos from Murmansk to Okhotsk. Time is too short. False moves have implications that are too dire. In many ways, the threats are even more real, the moves we have to make even more delicate, than when my uncle entered office 40 years ago. So, on January 21, 2001, who do you want in the Oval Office, a man who keeps a catalogue of those implications in his head, or a man who will have to learn them from scratch?

One last item from that day's paper.

In a test 140 miles above the Pacific Ocean, a $100 million test of the "Kill Vehicle" for our National Missile Defense System, a precursor to a $60 billion operational system, failed ("Kill Vehicle" – the Pentagon, seemingly redressing decades of euphemistically calling their weapons "Peacekeeper" or "Minuteman," seem to be wildly swinging back in the opposite direction). $100 million, down the drain. I know our country has invested massive amounts of our national treasure in the past – with very good reason – to ensure the safety and security of our people throughout the Cold War. But the Cold War is over and the threats to our safety and security more likely will come from a suitcase carried by a rogue terrorist roaming around downtown Manhattan than from an intercontinental ballistic missile launched from Baghdad.

And now we're out a $100 million, and we haven't made anyone any safer. If another arms race begins as a result, it will be just the opposite. Who, upon reading the news accounts of the test of our "Kill Vehicle," hasn't thought about how many real lives, this very day, could have been saved with that money? With this test behind us, it will most likely fall to the next president to make the decision about whether to spend the next $60 billion on this enterprise. I have no idea how President Gore would decide about such a weapon, though I'd give him my 2 cents if he asked. But I do know that President Bush would not build this system. He would build a more expensive one. Is that what we want?

Every newspaper stay that I have referenced here has taken place, obviously, on Bill Clinton's and Al Gore's watch. Harry Truman said that "the buck stops here" and with the many successes for which we are proud we cannot escape the many continuing difficulties and challenges for which we bear responsibility. But given the choice between taking on those challenges with a dedicated team that has invested eight years toward tackling them, or opting instead to anoint a new team that would summarily dismiss all the progress – and the continuing work for which we can take due pride – I think that the choice is clear.

Al Gore knows that there are many bridges yet to cross. George W. Bush does not know where the bridges are. I want to share just a few of my personal experiences from working on some of those bridges at home and abroad.

I participated this spring in the Million Mom March, where hundreds of thousands of mothers and other concerned citizens walked on Washington to demand stronger gun control and safety measures. The march grew out of citizen activism at a time when the political arena has failed to address one of the most pervasive evils in our society. On a beautiful day on the Mall, old and young, black and white, male and female, Christian and Jew, united in a cause. It was a cause with which I am all too familiar.

For me, the march was acutely important because my father was killed by a man with a handgun. But the implications of the march itself go far beyond people's personal motivations, or the terrible scourge that violence places on our society. The march demonstrates the power of ordinary citizens to change the course of events. It is a noble tradition as old as our nation's history, a tradition that has had its highs and lows during the last century, but which is seeing a rebirth – from our front yards to the farthest reaches of the Internet – as a century begins anew. And that is cause for hope and celebration.

Speaking out about it is the first step. Now is the time for action, with leadership from the White House and Capitol Hill and state capitals from Augusta to Sacramento. Bill Clinton started it and Al Gore should continue it. Where Clinton succeeded, Gore should build on it. Where Clinton failed,

Gore should pick up the pieces and rededicate his efforts. Nothing should come in the way of eliminating gun violence from our land and those that stand in the way do an injustice to us all.

I have kept a keen watch around the world, trying to understand the nature of civil and human rights and how and why they are abused. I watched the war crimes tribunal for Serbian atrocities. I have watched Truth Commission for South Africa. I have watched the toppling of scores of totalitarian regimes, from Romania to Indonesia, where rights have been trampled but now are being reborn.

I have asked myself, and you should too – what do these events mean for us, as Americans? As members of the world community, who are we? And where do we stand? The conservatives talk of compassion, but where is their compassion for issues like these? Walt Whitman wrote: "These States are the amplest poem. Here is not merely a nation, but a teeming nation of nations." That is what we are: A "nation of nations," and only one party truly embraces this.

For the women and men who conceived our "nation of nations," it meant a sense of commitment and courage which is, today, hard for us to imagine. Their commitment was to forge a nation from the dreams of those immigrants who arrived on its shores. Whether they were escaping poverty or oppression, these people who left their countries, their families, their friends or their possessions shared a faith that there was something better that awaited them in this new land. They sacrificed everything for it.

All Americans, as Franklin Roosevelt said, "are immigrants or descendants of immigrants." Even American Indians, who migrated here in our continent's distant past, or African-Americans, who arrived in manacles, belong in our "nation of nations" family, despite the injustices dealt them by later generations of immigrants. Imagine their collective courage on their voyage here, however they may have come. That courage is our common heritage, mustered by every woman, child and man who ventured to America.

It was a courage shared by people such as John Winthrop from England, Alexander Hamilton from the West Indies, Alexander Graham Bell from Scotland, Albert Einstein from Germany. More recently, it was a courage shared by people such as Isabel Allende from Peru, Mikhail Baryshnikov from Russia, Zubin Mehta from India, Hakeem Olajuwon from Nigeria, I.M. Pei from China and Elie Weisel from Romania.

John Kennedy wrote about this shared identity of America when he described us as "a nation of people with the fresh memory of old traditions, who dared to explore new frontiers, people eager to build lives for themselves in a spacious society that did not restrict their freedom of choice and action." That vision, that faith, that determination, that bravery – the very fact that we are a nation of immigrants – has formed the heart of our self image, made us strong and made us a leader among nations.

Today, this shared legacy has an added dimension. At a time when we enjoy unprecedented worldwide influence, we have an unavoidable responsibility to exemplify all that is good about being a "nation of nations" because so many other nationalities cannot seem to do the same. In today's world, people who have coexisted for decades are warring like never before: the Serbs and the Albanians, the Tutsis and the Hutus, the Turks and the Kurds. The list goes on. The reasons for such fraternal violence is explained in 1 million different ways, but it comes down to anger, fear and bigotry hiding under an exaggerated patriotism known as nationalism.

This devotion to the interests of one group by the exclusion of others grows out of racial and economic tensions, many of which have festered for centuries. Since the 1930s, the smell of freedom, of overthrowing the old order, plus a vast spread of cheap weapons and technological information – hand guns, bombs, radios, planes, drugs – has changed everything.

The mantle of repression has been lifted, but long-suppressed tensions have exploded. This is what we saw in the Balkans, where each side calls itself a state in order to assure dominance over any hated or feared others within that entity. Carried to its logical extreme, no state will have to address minority rights – or tolerate dissent in any form. As much as the future holds hope, it also holds fear.

The bloodshed caused the world over by ethnic rivalries has created the most pressing human rights violations in human history. But the horror is not just "over there." Fear, hatred and distrust are sorry realities of American life. They always have been.

They allowed us to enslave Africans and African-Americans for 246 years.

They allowed us to deny women the right to vote for all but the last 70 years.

In the 1880s, U.S. immigration policy excluded Asians. In the 1920s, it excluded southern Europeans and Jews. And in the 1930s, Mexicans were targeted. My grandmother, Rose Kennedy, made a point of showing all of her grandchildren employment advertisements she had saved since her youth in Boston that read "No Irish need apply" to ensure that we would remember our great nation was so capable of doing things that were not great, that flew in the face of our common heritage.

During World War II, we forced 110,000 Americans of Japanese ancestry, who had broken no laws, into barren, isolated American concentration camps, even while their husbands and sons defended our country on the front lines overseas.

Before that conflict began, America's refusal in 1939 to grant refuge to a boatload of European Jews fleeing the onslaught of the Holocaust remains a black mark on our national conscience. The *St. Louis* was turned away from our shores after Germany's state-sanctioned program during *kristellnacht*. Most of the 930 Jews on board then perished in concentration camps. When we work to prevent such genocide today it is, in part, because we are so haunted by the mistakes of our past.

But not everyone accepts the responsibility we bear.

Legalized bigotry is a festering part of the dark side of the American spirit. It was exemplified by George Wallace in the '60s, Lindon LaRouche in the '70s, and Pat Robertson in the '80s. That tradition has been handed down to their successors – Rush Limbaugh, Louis Farrakhan and Pat Buchanan – who continue to practice it today.

Can we afford to forget that Pat Buchanan's last presidential platform included a plan to erect a Berlin wall along the Mexican border? As we watched the election last week of Vicente Fox as the first non-PRI President of Mexico in 71 years, is that the message we want to send to our neighbors?

These same voices said we had no business in the Balkans. They urge us so slam tight the doors, batten down the hatches, slash immigration, gut foreign aid, dismantle the government, increase access to handguns and expand the death penalty.

This is not just rhetoric. Immigrant-bashing sentiments were transposed into law in 1996 with devastating consequences.

Let me tell you about one case. A family in California adopted a toddler from Thailand. He grew up in America, studied at the public school, spent weekends at the baseball game with his dad and hung out at the mall. When he was 17, his parents applied for a passport and were told there was a technical glitch on the adoption papers.

While the papers were being sorted out at the immigration service, the boy turned 18. He went out with some friends one night, stole a car, went for a joy ride, got caught, confessed and plead guilty. But now he was not just a boy owning up to his transgression. Now he was an illegal alien who committed a felony in the United States. The immigration department sought his deportation. He exhausted all his appeals and was sent to Thailand, a country where he has no known relatives or ties and where he does not speak the language. In Thailand, this American-bred boy was the alien.

This is the sad, sorry consequence of those easily exploited by groundless fears that our country is being overrun by foreigners. How could we do such a thing?

In the area of access to affordable housing, the stories that I hear about racial profiling from my husband, who is the Secretary of Housing and Urban Development, are a throwback to the '60s. In the last year, HUD has placed a high priority on cracking down on racial profiling and has prosecuted more than 1000 violations.

Let me tell you about three of them.

A Portuguese woman in Missouri moved into a new home. A few weeks later, a seven-foot cross, engulfed in flames, appeared on her lawn. They thought she was African-American and they didn't want her there.

In an apartment complex in New Orleans, they sent blacks to one side of the complex, whites to the other. Each side has its own swimming pool with no access between the two. One pool whites only. One pool blacks only. Are we still in the '50s?

And in Buffalo, New York, a landlady was told "if you rent to a black, we'll blow up the apartment, and then we'll kill you and your family."

Those are the stories of private citizens. Too often, they get no help from the people we put in power, who breed racism with their exclusionary rhetoric.

Apparently more concerned with the color of people's skin than the content of their character, Senator Richard Shelby warned an all-white audience in his home state of Alabama that "we've had lax immigration policies in this country for too long … at the rate we're going, by the year 2040 Anglo-Saxon people will be only 40% of the population."

What difference does it make if we have a country where minorities are the majority? We were all the minority at one point in our history. We should want our leadership to be less concerned with pedigrees and more concerned with college degrees. We should want our leadership to be less concerned with bloodlines and more concerned with bloodshed. We should want our leadership to be less concerned with race and more concerned with peace. We should want our leadership to be less concerned with ancestry and more concerned with opportunity.

Unfortunately, Richard Shelby is not alone. Let me give you one instance that changed my life: a story of how one of our own governmental institutions institutionalized racism.

As a sophomore in college, quite a long time ago, I took an internship with Amnesty International. The first immigration case on which I worked involved a mother whose husband and daughter had been killed by security forces in El Salvador. The mother paid a smuggler $1,000 and headed north with her son, where they were picked up by INS officials just over the Texas border. First, mother and son were separated and thrown into a filthy, mosquito-infested detention center built on a swamp.

When the 7-year-old boy refused to cooperate with officials, two of his fingers were broken. A doctor volunteered to set the fracture, but the INS refused to permit the doctor to give treatment to the boy. Drinking water was rancid, meager rations were rotten and meat was infected by mold. It's hard to believe that this was America.

Finally, the illiterate, Spanish-speaking mother and her child were coerced into signing voluntary departure forms – in English – and summarily shipped back to El Salvador – back to the war, back to the death squads, away from freedom.

I was horrified that my country, the richest and most powerful country on earth, treated the most destitute with such disdain. I couldn't believe the INS policy reflected our values as a society. The treatment by U.S. authorities of this family was in contravention of international treaties that we had signed to protect persons fleeing political persecution. And, perhaps worse in the long run, it fomented a residing distrust, even hatred, of the United States by those who should have been our most supporters.

But as I said, that was a long time ago.

I am lucky to be living in a country born of revolution, where institutions are capable of change. Through the work of human rights groups, I learned that citizens can, and eventually dramatically do, reverse many of our worst policies. Ironically, it is precisely because we are a nation of immigrants, who have come to our country seeking change, with an abiding faith in the possibility of making a better life, that we have maintained institutions in which citizen activism is both possible and effective.

Our United States, founded on a set of immutable principles of fairness, perhaps more than any other country, has a responsibility to support the institutions that will protect human rights and the rights of immigrants and refugees in particular. It is for this reason that the words "We are endowed by our creator with certain unalienable rights" are the cornerstones of both our Declaration of Independence and of the Universal Declaration of Human Rights.

That resolve is part of the soul of this nation. Our heritage appeals to the good, the generous, and the instinct for fairness in all Americans. This instinct says we can make a difference, no matter how insurmountable the problems may seem. This instinct says mothers can join together to stop the violence of guns.

This instinct that engages us in the struggle for human rights echoes the ancient Greeks, who believed it was ennobling to take part in the life of the nation.

If we need any more inspiration, Americans, who sometimes can take our freedom for granted, would be wise to learn from the people of some nations who have tasted the spirit of freedom for a much shorter time. I'd like to tell you about one man who embodies that spirit, Peter Magubane.

Peter is not an American, but he knows what it means to build a new nation. One of the foremost photojournalists in South Africa, he was threatened, imprisoned, beaten and tortured for covering the horrors of apartheid.

Six years ago, the day after President Mandela's inauguration, Peter took me on a tour of Soweto, the slum where blacks were forced to live in unspeakable conditions under the apartheid regime. He showed me the houses pieced together from abandoned planks and tin cans and mud. He showed me the communal outhouses – which lacked plumbing – that were used by entire neighborhoods. He showed me the dangerous kerosene fires that so often burned out of control but which, without electricity, were the only means for cooking in the community.

After viewing the devastation, I asked what would change with Nelson Mandela's presidency. Peter answered: "Never again will my house be destroyed because I pointed a camera. Never again will I spend 536 days in solitary confinement because I took a picture. Never again will I take 17 bullets because I did my job."

Hearing Peter's story, we must ask ourselves: why on earth would people risk house burnings, broken limbs or torture and solitary confinement to be able to do their work? What is the source of their courage? What is their source of commitment?

All of those who survive torture and take up the cause of human rights, like Peter, who have never given in to the forces of futility or the temptation toward violence, inspire us to embrace our beliefs and hold fast to our dreams.

⤳

Whether you make your judgment on who to support this fall – and how hard you are going to work for that person – based on long-held beliefs about how they will treat every person's basic human rights, or whether you make your judgment by keeping a close eye on the newspaper and how things are going in our country, you final judgment – when you put it all together – should be the same. Democrats, hold fast to your dreams, to our dreams and to the courage and your commitment of our fellow countrymen, past and present, and make America, America again.

Democrats arrived in Los Angeles this summer for our national convention with a mixture of optimism, nostalgia and ambivalence. They carried with them optimism that our nation will affirm the many accomplishments of the Clinton/Gore years and will elect Vice-President Gore to succeed the man who selected him as his running mate eight years ago.

They will carry with them nostalgia for the end of Bill Clinton's term in office and, perhaps, if they are old enough, for the memory of that evening, 40 years ago, when the Democratic Party bestowed its nomination for president upon my uncle, John F. Kennedy.

And perhaps they will carry with them ambivalence for the possibility that, as political cycles go, America might want a change purely for change's sake, and will reject the strides our nation has taken over the last eight years to combat the challenges that confronted us – and confront us still – at home and abroad.

Thirty-five years ago, my father, Robert F. Kennedy, said "as long as America must choose, that long will there be a need and a place for the Democratic Party. We Democrats can run on our record but we cannot rest on it. We will win if we continue to take the initiative and if we carry the message of hope and action throughout the country. Alexander Smith once said, 'A man doesn't plant a tree for himself. He plants it for posterity.' Let us continue to plant, and our children shall reap the harvest. That is our destiny as Democrats." What he said in 1965 is no less true today.

It's too easy, inside the voting booth, to pull the lever with an eye toward change and forget the implications of doing so.

It's too easy to forget, in the voting booth, that three new Supreme Court

Justices will likely be appointed by the next occupant of the Oval Office, and how the laws of our land may change as a result. Farewell, Miranda warning. Goodbye, a woman's right to choose. It's too easy to forget, in the voting booth, how much progress can be turned back overnight.

It's too easy to forget, in the voting booth, the practical reality of what the Democratic Administration has been able to accomplish – slow at first, but with a profound pace through the Clinton years, even in the face of an opposition-led Congress. In modern times, switching management just as it is hitting stride, just as they have come so close to so much success, seems foolhardy at best, irresponsible at worst. But it's too easy to forget, in the voting booth, how often a party coming into office for the first time after eight years in exile can knocked off stride, especially during the first two years in office, for both Republicans and Democrats alike. We don't have those two years to train a new team.

It's too easy to forget, in the voting booth, that the real results of a Republican victory would mean a White House-led effort to abolish the U.S. Department of Education, a repeal of the minimum wage laws, a phase-out of the Social Security system, a repeal of the "motor-voter" law, an adoption of "American English" as the official language of the nation and an end to all forms of U.S. participation in the United Nations. It sounds extreme, but it comes directly from the Republican platform and it's too easy to forget in the voting booth.

My uncle was nominated in Los Angeles 40 years ago, and it would be gratifying to watch this summer as a candidate who embraces many of his ideals, Vice-President Gore, begins to cross the many bridges toward victory in November. But the political pendulum too easily can swing back 20 years instead of 40 years, when Washington began a 12-year diversion toward ballooning deficits, a hyperactive arms race and disregard for human and civil rights, both within our borders and on the farthest reaches of the planet.

So, instead of trumpeting how much we have accomplished, let us continue to focus on how many bridges we still have to cross, knowing that there is only one person, one party and one team that can effectively lead us over them. In Los Angeles, the balloons fell and the music may blared, but let us be on guard against too much optimism, too much nostalgia and, yes, too much ambivalence about political cycles and change "for change's sake." Really, there are too many bridges left to cross.

———

KERRY KENNEDY CUOMO

Kerry Kennedy Cuomo started working in the field of human rights in 1981 when she investigated abuses committed by U.S. immigration officials against refugees from El Salvador. Since then, her life has been devoted to the vindication of equal justice, to the promotion and protection of basic rights and to the preservation of the rule of law. Currently she is writing "Speak Truth to Power," a book of profiles of 50 human rights defenders around the world to be published by Random House in September, 2000. She has led 40 human rights delegations to 27 countries. At a time of diminished idealism and growing cynicism about public service, her life and lectures are testaments to the commitment to the basic values of human rights.

Kennedy Cuomo served a Executive Director and is now on the Board of Directors of the Robert F. Kennedy Memorial, a non-profit organization that addresses the problems of social justice. She ran three programs: The National Juvenile Justice Project, which helps cities create more effective and less costly programs for dealing with young offenders; The RFK Journalism and RFK Book Awards, known as the "poor people's Pulitzers", which recognize those authors who prod our conscience and expose the problems of the dispossessed; and the RFK Center for Human Rights, which she founded in 1988.

Kennedy Cuomo established the RFK Center for Human Rights to ensure the protection of rights codified under the U.N. Declaration of Human Rights. The Center provides an on going base of support to leading human rights defenders around the world. The Center uncovers and publicizes abuses such as torture, disappearances, repression of free speech and child labor; urges Congress and the U.S. administration to highlight human rights in foreign policy, supplies activists with the resources they need to advance their work and creates other programs to advance respect for human rights.

Kennedy Cuomo has led delegations to and negotiated with government officials from: Canada 1997, Colombia 1999; Costa Rica 1999, Czechoslovakia 1991; Czech Republic 1999; East Timor 1999; Egypt 1999; El Salvador 1989, 1992, 1999; Gaza 1994; Guatemala 1992, 1999; Haiti 1991; Hungary 1987, 1991; India 1998; Indonesia 1999:

Israel 1994; Ireland 1999; Japan 1993, 1994; Kenya 1989, 1993; Malawi 1993; Mexico 1994, 1999; Northern Ireland 1988, 1989, 1994, 1997; the Philippines 1992; Poland 1987, 1991; South Africa 1993, 1994; South Korea 1988, 1990, 1992; Spain 1999;Venezuela 1989; and the World Conference on Human Rights, Vienna, Austria, 1993. She has also supported human rights related causes in China, Indonesia, Vietnam, India, Sudan, Pakistan and other countries. She was an election observer in Chile during the 1988 plebiscite which ousted General Augusto Pinochet.

She has worked on diverse human rights issues such as child labor, disappearances, indigenous land rights, judicial independence, freedom of expression, ethnic violence, impunity, the environment and women's rights.

Kennedy Cuomo has appeared on ABC, NBC, CBS, CNN among others and her commentaries and articles have been published in The Boston Globe, The Chicago Sun-Times, The New York Times, TV Guide and the Yale Journal of International Law. As a special correspondent for the environmental magazine television program, "Network Earth," she reported on human rights and the environment. She interviewed human rights leaders for Voice of America.

Kennedy Cuomo is Chair of the Amnesty International Leadership Council and is a judge for the Reebok Human Rights Award. She serves on the boards of directors of Amnesty International, the International Center for Ethics, Justice and Public Life at Brandeis University, the Lawyers' Committee for Human Rights, the Bloody Sunday Trust and the Robert F. Kennedy Memorial, as well as the Gleitzman Foundation's Special Board of Advisors for the Sakharov Award and the Editorial Board of Advisors of the "Buffalo Human Rights Law Review." She is on the Advisory Committee for the National Coalition to Abolish the Death Penalty, the Committee on the Administration of Justice (Northern Ireland) and the International Campaign for Tibet. She is Co-Chair of the Board of Governors of SpeakOut.com. Kennedy Cuomo has served in numerous political campaigns and she is a member of the Massachusetts and District of Columbia bars.

Kerry Kennedy Cuomo is a graduate of Brown University and Boston College Law School. She is married to Secretary of Housing and Urban Development Andrew Cuomo with whom she has three girls, Cara, Mariah and Michaela.

CHAPTER FOUR

★

ALAN M.
DERSHOWITZ

NO RELIGIOUS TEST...

*I*n 1790, President George Washington assured the tiny Jewish community in Newport, Rhode Island that, "It is now no more that toleration is spoken of, as if it was by the indulgence of one class of people, that another enjoyed the exercise of their inherent natural rights." Instead he promised that in America, all religious groups would be treated equally. It may have taken many decades for the seeds of Constitutional equality to blossom into the flower of real equality, but America has long been on the forefront of providing the equal protection of the laws. Our Constitution provides that no religious test shall ever be required for holding office in the United States, but over the years an informal religious test prevailed. In 1928, the Democratic Party cast aside that religious test by nominating a Catholic to run for President of the United States. He lost the election. In 1960, after the Democrats once again nominated a Catholic, the American people categorically rejected religious disqualification for high office. Again, in 1984 the Democratic Party broke an informal barrier, this time by nominating a woman, also a Catholic, for Vice-President. And now in 2000, the Democratic Party has challenged the conventional wisdom that only a Christian can be President of the United States, by nominating an Orthodox Jew to run for Vice-President.

It is interesting to note that these precedent-shattering challenges to bigotry have come from the Democratic Party. Every single Republican nominee for President has been a white, Anglo-Saxon, Protestant male (one Republican Vice-Presidential nominee, William Miller in 1964, was Catholic). This Republican white, Protestant, male exclusivity too shall come to an end in the years to come, but it will not be easy, as evidenced by the fact that the Republican majority in the Senate has repeatedly blocked the nominations of qualified African-Americans and Asians for federal judgeships and other high positions.

Nor have all the barriers yet been eliminated, even by the Democratic Party. Is the nation willing to accept an eminently qualified African-American candidate for the presidency or vice-presidency? What about an eminently qualified gay American? Muslim-American? Asian-American? In theory, the answer is yes. Even the polls appear encouraging, though all pollsters recognize that some people tend to hide their bigotry, even from pollsters, but vote them in the anonymity of the polling booth.

Among the great struggles that America confronts in the 21st century is to bring about true equality, in practice as well as in theory. We will never be the great nation that we ought to be until all barriers based on race, religion, ethnicity, national origin, sexual orientation, economic status, class, physical disability and other invidious classifications have been eliminated. An editorial cartoon by Wasserman shows a future presidential candidate introducing his vice-presidential nominee an atheist. This could not happen in America today, despite our constitutional prohibition against religious tests, because most Americans falsely assume that only religious people can be moral. America must lead the way toward complete equality and diversity, and only the

Democrats can lead America, because the Republican Party founded by Lincoln has all but abandoned the heritage out of which it was born.

One necessary step toward full equality is electoral reform. So long as elections can be bought by largely unregulated and self-serving campaign contributions from the wealthiest corporate interests, our theoretical commitment to one person, one vote will remain an illusion. Everyone has the right to cast a vote, but the reality is that only the rich have the power to buy the votes of those whose decisions are based on which candidate can purchase the most access to the media.

There is a wonderful story of an Eastern European rabbi in the 18th century who was asked by the synagogue president whether it would be proper to have a system of weighted voting under which the largest contributors to the synagogue were given the most votes in synagogue matters. The rabbi responded that weighted voting was permissible so long as it served the interests of ultimate equality of all members. Thus, he proposed that those members who make the largest contributions would get the smallest number of votes and those members who could not afford to make large contributions would be allotted the greatest number of votes. The rabbi said that this plan would recognize the reality that those who contribute the most money already have the most influence on synagogue policy through their contributions and that in order to level the playing field, the poorest would have to be given extra votes. I am not suggesting that we follow the rabbi's prescription for affirmative action in voting, but I am suggesting that we eliminate the enormous disparity that comes with virtually unlimited campaign contributions. Yes, contributions are a kind of speech, but they are the kind of speech that silences others and are therefore subject to Constitutional regulation in the interest of opening up the channels of Democracy and implementing our policy of equality.

Other areas of inequality that must be addressed are education, health care and access to our growing economic benefits. The gaps in these areas are growing and that is not a prescription for political stability. As technology advances, the need for an excellent education becomes even more important.

As health care improves, it is imperative that longevity not become a matter of class or race. As business booms, those at the margins of our economy must not be left behind.

One problem that neither the Democrats nor the Republicans are sufficiently addressing is our growing prison population. Never before in American history have so many people been subject to imprisonment and other forms of confinement. Most of these prisoners are non-violent and come from the most marginalized segments of our society. Winston Churchill was right when he said: "The mood and temper of the public in regard to the treatment of crime and criminals is one of the most unfailing tests of the civilization of any country. A calm dispassionate recognition of the rights of the accused and even of the convicted criminal against the state; a constant heart-searching of all charged with the deed of punishment; tireless efforts towards the discovery of regenerative processes; unfailing faith that there is a treasure, if you can find it, in the heart of every man. These are the symbols which in the treatment of crime and criminals make and measure the stored-up strength of a nation and are sign and proof of the living virtue in it." Our burgeoning prison population is a mirror of our failure to bring about full equality of opportunity. But neither the Democratic nor the Republican Party want to be perceived as being on the side of criminals, as distinguished from the victims. But the reality is that the criminals and the victims generally come from the same background and economic status. We must address the conditions that lead both to victimization and to criminality, without reducing our security and the need to be protected from those who would prey on others.

We are too close to becoming a truly great society to become complacent. The struggle for equality never stays won. It is an ongoing and ever-changing process. We are a country of immigrants. Most of our forbearers were marginalized members of the communities from which they emigrated. They sought the American dream a dream that must not be denied to others. We must vote our memories as well as our aspirations.

ALAN M. DERSHOWITZ

A Brooklyn native who has been called *"the nation's most peripatetic civil liberties lawyer,"* and *"the best-known criminal lawyer in the world,"* ALAN M. DERSHOWITZ is the Felix Frankfurter Professor of Law at Harvard Law School. Dershowitz, a graduate of Brooklyn College and Yale Law School, joined the Harvard Law School faculty at age 25 after clerking for Judges David Bazelon and Arthur Goldberg.

While he is known for defending clients such as Anatoly Sharansky, Claus von Bülow, O.J. Simpson, Michael Milken and Mike Tyson, he continues to represent numerous indigent defendants and takes half of his cases pro bono.

Dershowitz is the author of a dozen fiction and non-fiction works. His writing has been praised by Truman Capote, Saul Bellow, David Mamet, William Styron, Aharon Appelfeld, A.B. Yehoshua and Elie Wiesel. More than a million of his books have been sold worldwide.

His most recent nonfiction title is *"The Genesis of Justice: Ten Stories of Biblical Injustice that Led to the Ten Commandments and Modern Law."* His most recent novel is *"Just Revenge."* Dershowitz is also the author of *"The Vanishing American Jew," "The Abuse Excuse," "Reasonable Doubts," "Chutzpah"* (a #1 bestseller), *"Reversal of Fortune"* (which was made into an Academy Award-winning film), *"Sexual McCarthyism"* and *"The Best Defense"* .

CHAPTER FIVE

★

CHAZ HAMMELSMITH
EBERT

CHOOSING OUR FUTURE

*W*hen I think about the most compassionate political party, I think about the Democrats. When I think about the party of the people, the Democrats come to mind. When I ask myself who is more likely to create legislation that will allow for the best opportunity for the most people in this society to fulfill the ideal of the American Dream including housing, education, work and the pursuit of happiness, I think of the Democrats. And quite frankly, when I ponder who will continue to carry out environmental legislation to make sure this nation has clean air, clean water and properly disposed of hazardous waste, I think of Vice-President, Al Gore. That is why I am a Democrat and why I actively support local and national candidates in the Democratic Party.

I guess I was taught to be a Democrat at my parents' knees. Mother, Mrs. Johnnie Mae Hammel, whom we all called Big Mama, was a precinct captain, and I remember knocking on many doors with her to get people to go out to vote. Father, Mr. Wiley James Hammel, told us about the horror of poll taxes, literacy tests, threats and intimidation and other discriminatory hindrances to voting he encountered while growing up in the South. Once while Daddy and I were marching with Dr. Martin Luther King Jr., Daddy looked me in the eye and told me that too many people sacrificed so much to gain the privilege of voting, that I was never to take it for granted. And I don't.

Webster's New World dictionary defines a democrat as: 1. A person who believes in and upholds government by the people. 2. A person who believes in and practices the principle of equality of rights, opportunity and treatment. And I have high hopes for the Democratic Party. I want to strive for a nation, economically secure, where children can thrive and grow and get a good education in their public schools. Where their parents can find meaningful work under fair conditions, knowing they can get the type of support they need through available child care and health care programs. Where families can meet and greet each other without hiding out behind their doors because of the crime in their communities fueled by the drug trade. Where alcoholics and addicts can be rehabilitated and returned as productive members of their communities. And where employment discrimination based on race, sex, age, physical disability or sexual orientation will not be tolerated.

In searching for a way to have more of a voice in the shaping of issues and values for the Democratic party, I chaired a town hall meeting in Chicago in conjunction with the Women's Leadership Forum where we invited First Lady Hillary Rodham Clinton to speak. Fundraising is a political necessity, but adding a more grassroots, networking and empowering event like the town hall meeting stirred my visceral fire and passion and re-awakened the belief that we can make a difference. We reached out to diverse women in the community, in some cases to women who had never actively participated in the political process. As I listened to the dialogue between Mrs. Clinton and the audience of smart, capable women about issues like breaking through the glass ceiling, education, gun control, the right to choose whether or not to have a child without government intrusion and other issues, I couldn't help but think that if you want to have a voice, you have to "do something." And if you want to "do something" on what you feel is the correct side of these issues, you have to "do something" with the Democratic Party.

A particular incident comes to mind. I had the privilege of serving on the Democratic Site Selection Committee to survey different cities in order to choose where the Year 2000 Democratic National Convention would be held. One of the cities we surveyed was Philadelphia. The members of the committee had all rearranged their schedules to go to Philadelphia, but when we arrived there was a strike by the transit workers union. What should we do? The consensus of the group was that we could not cross the picket lines. We decided to return at a more opportune time. And as the daughter of an old union man, I couldn't have felt better about our decision. Daddy would have been proud of us. The Democrats are traditionally the friends of the labor unions. We knew that the Republicans were also considering Philadelphia as their convention city, so we were curious about how they had handled the strike situation. We heard that they took the opposite track. They crossed the picket lines.

I guess some of this sounds idealistic and unrealistic. Well, actually, I am a realist, but I also think we have to reach for the stars. I love the fact that the Democratic party is a party of inclusiveness, not divisiveness. We think the boat is big enough to accommodate black and white, brown and yellow and red. We are a party of equal opportunity, not snobbery or discrimination. We want to provide an atmosphere where each member of society can fulfill his or her full potential. And we think that is the way to achieve the common good; a party of the people, by the people and for the people, with liberty and justice for all.

CHAZ HAMMELSMITH EBERT

Chaz Hammelsmith Ebert is Vice-President of The Ebert Company. Previously, as a civil rights attorney she was named Lawyer of the Year by the Constitutional Rights Foundation and was selected as one of the Outstanding Women in America. She also has practiced in the fields of environmental law with the EPA; employment discrimination law with the EEOC; and commercial and business litigation, including mergers and acquisitions and antitrust law with the law firm of Bell, Boyd & Lloyd.

Her civic and community passions include an interest in programs for children and families with an emphasis on education and the arts; and advocating business opportunities for women to help shatter the glass ceiling.

She has a Bachelors degree in Political Science from the University of Dubuque; a Master's degree in Social Science from the University of Wisconsin; and a law degree from DePaul University.

CHAPTER SIX

★

STEVE GROSSMAN

DEMOCRACY AND DEMOCRATS
AT THE MILLENNIUM

★

s the 20th century drew to a close last year, pundits proclaimed it "democracy's century." The first truly democratic country was not Greece in the 5th century B.C., England in 1215 or even the United States in 1776. At the turn of the 20th century, not one country granted its citizens universal suffrage. Believe it or not, the first country to elect its government on the principle of universal suffrage in multiparty, competitive elections was Finland in 1906.

Less than a hundred years later, there are 119 democratic countries – almost 2/3rds of the world's nations containing 3/5ths of its people. For the first time in history, a majority of the world's people live under governments of their own choosing. Democracy can now be said to be a universal human value, a system of government and a set of principles underpinning it that are aspired to by the vast majority of people around the globe. Franklin Roosevelt's articulation of those principles in 1941 as the "Four Freedoms" helped make them the world's ideals: freedom of speech, freedom of worship, freedom from want and freedom from fear.

I believe that the 20th century was also the Democratic Party's century. The vision of 20th century Democratic Presidents like Woodrow Wilson, Franklin Roosevelt, Harry Truman, John F. Kennedy, Lyndon Johnson, Jimmy Carter and Bill Clinton gave light and hope to people not only in the United States but around the world. And they presided over a party composed of a remarkable and changing coalition of disparate and sometimes conflicting groups and interests, a coalition that has reflected the complexity and diversity of the world around it: farmers, veterans, urban immigrants, union labor, consumer-oriented businessmen, liberal intellectuals, Catholics, Jews, Southerners, blacks, etc. Inclusion has been not only a cardinal principle for the Democratic Party, it has been a way of life.

I was privileged to serve from 1997 to 1999 as national chairman of the Democratic National Committee, which is now the oldest continuous political party organization on the face of the earth. Thomas Jefferson's "party of the common man," organized as the DNC in 1848 after Andrew Jackson's presidency reunited fractured Democrats, has survived and thrived because of its remarkable capacity to embrace the changing American electorate.

In the words of the late party chairman Ron Brown, "The common thread of Democratic history, from Thomas Jefferson to Bill Clinton, has been an abiding faith in the judgment of hard-working American families, and a commitment to helping the excluded, the disenfranchised and the poor strengthen our nation by earning themselves a piece of the American Dream. We remember that this great land was sculpted by immigrants and slaves, their children and grandchildren."

At the turn of the 20th century, the Democratic Party recognized the immigrants flooding across our borders as the source of new political power and activism in America – and more importantly, that their values resonated with the Party's. In my home state of Massachusetts, the legendary Democratic political boss Martin Lomasney used to stand on the docks in Boston holding a sign printed in many languages, inviting new arrivals from Ireland, Italy and many other nations to join his political club and his political party.

My grandfather, Max Grossman, was one of those attracted into the Democratic Party community. He came to East Boston as a small child at the turn of the century, with a family searching – like so many others – for freedom from want and freedom from intolerance. His parents were poor and he had to leave school in the 6th grade to go to work shining shoes on a ferry-boat. A few years later, when he was a teenager casting about on the streets looking for a way to pass the time, a friend brought him along to a Democratic Club meeting and he was hooked for life.

Max Grossman started out working on the mayoral re-election campaign of John "Honey" Fitzgerald, President Kennedy's grandfather, in 1910. After he established a successful business and his family's economic future was secure, he turned the company over to his two sons and devoted the rest of his life to politics and public service. He worked as a "dollar-a-year man" in FDR's administration under John Kenneth Galbraith, helped James Michael Curley get elected mayor of Boston for a fourth term in 1945, served as a delegate with my father to the 1948 Democratic National Convention in Philadelphia and eventually served both as penal commissioner for the city of Boston and as commissioner of correction for the Commonwealth of Massachusetts.

I reflected frequently over the course of 1999 on the story of my family during the 20th century, a story repeated over and over in so many families all across America. The last time I saw my grandfather in 1963, he summed up his life for me by saying that he only ever wanted to do four things: have a healthy family, educate his children, start his own business so he wouldn't have to depend on someone else for his livelihood and give something back to the community – in his case, the Democratic Party – that threw him a lifeline when he needed it. Despite all the change that has occurred over the course of this amazing century, I believe these are the things that we still value most highly and that the Democratic Party stands for most emphatically: healthy families, education, economic opportunity, and building community.

A year-end editorial in the New York Times proclaimed, "…the surest way to reach across time is through the transmission of enduring values and ideals." From the Greek and Enlightenment philosophers to Washington and Jefferson to Vaclav Havel and Nelson Mandela. And from my grandparents to my parents to me to my children. If the Democratic Party is to survive and thrive in the future, it must also transmit its values and ideals in new ways to new generations of citizens.

This will be no mean feat, for political parties – and democracy itself – are suffering the effects of citizen apathy and indifference.

In 1993 I was privileged to sit with Yitzhak Rabin in Jerusalem on the day the Oslo accords became known to the world. He knew he was taking an enormous political risk in supporting the agreement. But he also knew that Palestinians as well as Israelis needed to be free from want and from fear in order for democratic institutions to flourish and that those healthy institutions were a precondition for peace. He told me that when people have virtually no income, no way of providing for their families, are ill-clothed and ill-fed, have limited health care and little hope that tomorrow will be better than today, they have no stake in the success of the democratic process. Unrest and violence are likely to fill that void.

My good friend Lenny Zakim, who was New England Regional Director of the Anti-Defamation League until he succumbed to cancer last December, taught me that we must be tireless in confronting and resisting injustice and intolerance, but we must be equally passionate about confronting and resisting apathy, which he saw as a much more pernicious and widespread evil. In the immortal words of the British statesman Edmund Burke, "The only thing necessary for the triumph of evil is for good men to do nothing."

As a new century dawns, I have some concerns about the health of our "cradle of liberty." In a democracy the people are the source of power, but they must participate to wield that power. We have seen a precipitous decline in political participation in America. More than 60 percent of the total voting-age population cast a ballot in the 1960s, while only 36 percent did in 1998; in 1996 turnout was lower than it has been in a presidential election year since 1924. Voter turnout in most of the established democracies around the world averages 77 percent — more than twice as high as it was in the U.S. in 1998. The U.S. ranks 139th in the world in average voter turnout since 1945 – in the bottom 20 percent of nations in the world.

Trust in government and its leaders is also at historic lows in this country. In 1964, ¾ths of Americans said they trusted the federal government to do the right thing; today only ¼th do.

While the solutions to cynicism and apathy among the electorate are far from obvious or straightforward, I believe there are some things we can do to breathe new life into participatory democracy. For example, we're still voting the same way we did in the 18th century, when we were a largely agrarian society that ran on the harvest calendar. Today, people work long hours and frequently at more than one job. At home, they care for young children and aging parents. Innovations in the voting process such as weekend voting – which helps make possible the high turnout in nations such as France and Australia – same-day registration and mail balloting make it possible for more people to get to the polls and participate in the process. USA Today found that almost 60 percent of Americans polled were more likely to vote if they could vote on weekends.

Skeptics abound, but I believe that Internet voting will also be a viable option soon. Many experts believe that improvements in on-line security make Internet voting a real possibility today. As IBM chairman and CEO Louis Gerstner recently wrote, "It's time to harness technology to the service of democracy." Tens of millions of Americans surf the Internet regularly and the number of personal computers capable of Internet access is growing worldwide, from fewer than 60 million in 1996 to an estimated 256 million in 2000. If we want to encourage consistent voting from an early age, we must connect with young Americans where they gather – on the Internet. Online voting would also enhance access to the ballot for tens of millions of Americans with disabilities.

Though I believe Internet voting should be only one of a variety of methods available to citizens, I do share the concerns of those who warn of the effects of the "digital divide." Low-income families are far less likely to have access to the Internet and computers. African-American and Latino families are ⅖ths as likely to have home Internet access as white families. Bridging this divide must be a national priority over the next five to ten years, given the astounding growth in America's Internet economy and the premium placed by employers on workers skilled in using information technology. Internet access must become as inexpensive and ubiquitous as telephone service, and I believe it will, especially if we keep a Democratic President in the White House. Technologies are morphing rapidly and prices are dropping precipitously and I believe that it won't be long before virtually every household has some form of access to the Internet, the way virtually every household has a television today.

Re-engaging young people and bringing new voters into the process are also critical for a revitalized democracy. The College Democrats report that turnout of young people has been declining steadily during the 1990s. In Massachusetts alone, 50,000 young people turn 18 every year – that's 500,000 potential new voters over the next 10 years. We can't afford to have those young people, with their energy and idealism, turn away from the political process. A Close Up Foundation survey of high school students last year showed that while they are enthusiastic about volunteering in their communities, they are increasingly uninterested in pursuing careers related to politics, volunteering for a political campaign or even writing to an elected official. We must make politics and public service exciting, relevant and honorable again.

A thornier challenge than many of these, but one we absolutely must meet, is real and comprehensive campaign finance reform. Too many people believe the system is bought and paid for by wealthy corporations and individuals, and that their participation and votes mean nothing. Breathtaking amounts of money are spent on a "product" – the political process – that fewer and fewer "consumers" are buying. In any business, this would be a clear sign of something profoundly wrong. In politics, a military metaphor seems more appropriate: we seem to have fought each other to a standstill on the battlefield – the democratic process has been reduced to "Mutually Assured Destruction."

The Guardian editorialized at year-end, "This has been the century of the activist, when the age-old grip of the few on political life was finally broken. … The many had arrived on the political stage. … If current trends were to continue," however, "politics would once again become a specialized function reserved for elites, their relationship with the public governed by the media. But forcing the genie of political participation back into the bottle for good is likely to prove an impossible task."

Politicians always say that they are in favor of increasing citizen participation and voter turnout, but in reality many would rather keep the genie in the bottle. They favor turning out *their* voters, the ones they have identified who will vote for *them*. Political campaigns have become as much a science as an art and predictability is the highest value. The conventional wisdom says that you don't waste your time with young people, new immigrants, etc. because they have not historically voted in significant numbers.

But in the long term, I believe this is a losing strategy for the Democratic Party. We are at a moment when the old ways and certainties are beginning to crumble. Times change and just as we can't vote the way we used to, we can't organize the way we used to. So many voters are independent, unaffiliated, disengaged and cynical that we are beginning to lose our ability to predict and control the results of elections; our "base" is shrinking. We have to acknowledge that the electorate is changing in profound ways, as it changed at the turn of the 20th century. What would have happened to our Party if the Martin Lomasneys of the world had listened to the people who undoubtedly told him, "Don't waste your time on those people – they'll never vote"? We would have missed the opportunity to bring generations into the process.

The election of 1992 was the first in which voters who identified themselves as "independent" formed a plurality of the electorate and their numbers are growing. In Massachusetts – still thought of as a rock-solid Democratic state – "unenrolleds," as they're called, now make up a more than half of all voters.

The election of Jesse Ventura as Governor of Minnesota in 1998 was an object lesson in the perils of business-as-usual for political parties. In a poll done by the *Minneapolis Star Tribune* six weeks before the election, the Democratic candidate had 49 percent of the vote, the Republican 29 percent, and Ventura only 10 percent. On November 4 the citizens of Minnesota woke up to find they had a professional wrestler as their new governor. How could the poll have been so wrong? For one thing, it counted only people who had voted in the past. Ventura brought people to the polls who hadn't voted for years – or ever in their lives. Twelve percent said they showed up only because Ventura was on the ballot. Minnesota easily led the nation in the percentage of eligible voters who participated that year.

The parties responded to Ventura's election by railing against same-day registration, which many believed was responsible for his victory. In California that same year, the parties tried to close the state's open presidential primary, a move that California voters rejected. I fear these responses only contribute to the public's feeling of alienation from political parties, to an impression that they are self-serving, bureaucratic organizations out of sync with citizens' values and priorities.

I strongly believe we must have a proactive, not a reactive strategy – one that is based on the Democratic Party's strong foundation of coalition-building, bringing people together around a common set of principles and goals. Another thing Lenny Zakim taught me is that politics is all about relationships, and that building coalitions with potential friends and allies is an "ongoing responsibility and a continuing opportunity."

If the Democratic Party is to grow and flourish in the 21st century, we must find new ways to make people feel that their personal energy, activism and passion are valued in politics. We have to create new opportunities and access points within the organization. And we must start with young people – not just voting-age kids, but high school students.

The Democratic Party needs not only to take advantage of the energy and passion of young people as campaign workers but to give them positions of leadership and take their input seriously. And it has to start at the level of ward, town and city committees. I have spent a lot of time over the last year with Democratic committees all over the state of Massachusetts. The average age of their members is rising and most of them know they need an infusion of younger activists to replenish their ranks and take over the reins in the coming years. Grassroots organizations need to open up, to share power with newcomers – to put another leaf in the table, if you will.

I have encountered so many extraordinary young people who have so much to offer the Party and are just looking for a receptive audience. Last year, for example, I met a young man named Jonathan Sclarsic who was about to graduate from high school and head to Brandeis University. Through the Young Democrats of Massachusetts (YDM), he is beginning to organize Democratic clubs in high schools around the state, reasoning that giving young people a sense of the excitement and possibilities of politics at the earliest possible age will make them more likely to register to vote when they turn 18. And I believe they will be more likely to register as Democrats, because they will know that Democrats share their values and because Democrats reached out to them and made them part of something. Jonathan is Vice-President and Campaign Director of the College Democrats of Massachusetts, the head of the student senate at Brandeis and is currently managing a campaign for state representative. He is clearly on a fast-track career path of service to the Democratic Party.

The College Democrats of America have embarked on an ambitious plan to establish 500 new chapters on campuses around the country in this election cycle. But more than increasing their numbers, their goal is to make sure that the message disseminating from the Democratic Party is motivating young Americans to exercise their civic responsibility to vote. The good news is that Democrats have stood firmly with young people on the issues of most immediate concern to them: job security, the ability to pay student loans, car payments, housing and health insurance, etc. We need to make sure that we're delivering that message in ways and places that young people will hear it.

There has also been a surge of activism within constituencies that represent the future of our democracy and the Democratic Party needs to once again reach out to and give these new sources of political power a seat at the table. The Census estimates that by the middle of this century black, Hispanic and Asian-Pacific Americans will comprise more than 187 million of the 403 million people living in this country – nearly half. We are truly well on our way to becoming the first truly multi-racial, multi-ethnic democracy humankind has ever created. Across the country, Hispanics are the fastest-growing minority group and are projected to be the largest by 2005. They are sometimes referred to as the "Sleeping Giant" in politics, implying that their power is dormant. But in 1998, voter turnout declined in every demographic group except among Hispanic; certainly one of the primary reasons that Democrats did as well as they did in the '98 elections was because of the participation of the Hispanic electorate.

I also believe that Democrats need to refocus their attentions on the cities of America. I am convinced that the story of the next decade will be the revival of the cities in this country – economically, culturally and politically – that had been largely written off. New waves of immigrants to urban centers are finding their political voice and establishing their economic power. People are beginning to move back to the cities from the suburbs as crime has declined and as suburban sprawl and its attendant ills – traffic, pollution, etc. – increase.

Democrats also need to do better job of understanding how the New Economy is changing the workforce and its political orientation and priorities. "Knowledge workers" are becoming an increasingly large component of the workforce. There are now more self-employed Americans than Americans in labor unions. About 44 million Americans are working at least part-time from home. This is the subject of a whole chapter, if not a book, of its own, but suffice it to say that it's critical we focus on these changing realities now.

And finally, just as the Internet can be a powerful tool for re-engaging people with their democratic institutions, it can also be a powerful tool for political organizing. So far not many candidates or parties have used it as much more than a vehicle for posting the online equivalent of brochures. But if a great campaign is about building and communicating with webs or networks of people and relationships, often across wide geographic areas, what better tool could there be than the network of all networks, the Internet?

In the world of Internet business, it's said you have to "change or die." So many changes have occurred in our democracy over the last century demographically and technologically. What hasn't changed is the values that bring us together and the urgency of participating in the process.

The greatest risk is always not taking one. I'll take my chance in the marketplace of ideas that Democrats will win the votes of young people, of ethnic minorities, of knowledge workers, etc. if we speak to them clearly about their values and priorities. During the 1990s Democrats learned economics, learned the importance of fiscal responsibility, but Republicans did not learn compassion. At a time when people feel prosperous, but also find it increasingly difficult to balance work and family life, at a time when people are doing well economically but do not feel entirely confident about what the future holds for themselves or their children, polls show they trust Democrats over Republicans to protect their interests. Voters may continue to register as independents, but they will always reward candidates who are receptive to their interests.

New York Times columnist Thomas Friedman reflected in his January 1, 2000 essay on the incredible change that our world is going through at warp speed. "This may be the millennium," he wrote, "but it's no time for us to get old." He invoked the lyrics of Bob Dylan's ballad "Forever Young" as he hoped that America could "revive that youthful, radically creative spirit" that was the genius of our founders: "May your hands always be busy / May your feet always be swift / May you have a strong foundation when the winds of changes shift / And may you stay forever young."

STEVEN GROSSMAN

Steve Grossman is President of MassEnvelopePlus in Somerville, Massachusetts, a full-service printing and graphic design firm started by his grandfather in 1910 that has grown from a $4 million to a $30 million enterprise since he joined it in 1969. He is also Founder and President of Givenation.com, an Internet company designed to help nonprofit organizations raise funds online.

Grossman has played a prominent role in national and state politics, most recently as National Chairman of the Democratic National Committee from 1997 to 1999, which he helped revitalize after the 1996 election cycle, cutting the party's debt from $20 million to $5 million and laying the groundwork for the Democrats' stunning *success in the 1998 elections. Grossman also served as President and Chairman of the Board of the American Israel Public Affairs Committee (AIPAC) from 1992-1996 and Chairman of the Massachusetts Democratic Party from 1991-1992. A strong believer in the power of grassroots politics, he remains an active member of the Ward 7 Newton Democratic City Committee.*

Grossman also has been a leader of many philanthropic, civic and cultural organizations over the years. He currently serves as Chairman of the Board of Trustees of Brandeis University and sits on more than a dozen other boards, including the Boston Museum of Fine Arts, Children's Hospital, Combined Jewish Philanthropies of Greater Boston, the Anti-Defamation League of B'nai B'rith, Facing History and Ourselves National Foundation and the Robert F. Kennedy Memorial. He is the recipient of numerous honors and awards, including The Labor Guild's Cushing-Gavin Award, the Annual Brotherhood Award from the National Conference for Community and Justice and the National Jewish Democratic Council's Hubert H. Humphrey Humanitarian Award.

Grossman graduated from Princeton University in 1967 with an AB Cum Laude in Romance Languages and received his MBA from Harvard Business School in 1969 where he was a Baker Scholar. He is married to Dr. Barbara W. Grossman, a theater historian and a professor at Tufts University. Barbara and Steve have three sons, David, Benjamin and Joshua.

CHAPTER SEVEN

DELORIS
JORDAN

"EVEN A BLIND MAN SHOULD BE ABLE TO SEE…"

*t*he Clinton/Gore administration has made a big difference to our country and particularly to our economy. Social security, health care, education, funding for scholarships and day care — all these programs have found new life under the present administration. Even a blind man should be able to see how the economy has turned around in this country for all people of all cultures. In fact, to anyone who has had the chance to participate in this society and has not been able to grow and profit from it, I have to say, there must be something wrong with you.

Because of my son Michael's great success, I've been given the opportunity to see things first hand that other people may not. I've seen the changes right here on the West Side of Chicago, a low-income community, at the James Jordan Boys and Girls Club, with which I am closely involved. I've seen the increased funding they've received under Clinton and Gore, and I've seen the difference it has made. I've also traveled all over the world, even as far as Israel, where I had the opportunity to meet with the mayor of Jerusalem, and I've seen the good things that have been happening in other countries because of our support.

All my life, my family has come first. Even when I was working outside the home, as I did for 13 years, my top priority was always my children and I told that to my employer. I didn't take lunch hours so that I could leave early to participate in school activities. All their teachers and counselors, the people at our church, the whole community knew that Mrs. Jordan was their partner when it came to anything having to do with the children. Raising children is hard work. It requires dedication and staying focused — every day. And it's important to build that network of community relationships that provide you with a support system. I've been lucky enough to be given the chance to talk to parents all over the country about my beliefs and it has been extremely fulfilling to be able to bring them information, and hope, and new ways to think about things.

I know that Vice-President and Mrs. Gore, as well as President and Mrs. Clinton understand the importance of educating parents so that they can, in turn, educate their children about the importance of the *real* family values. I first met Vice-President Gore five years ago, after I wrote my book, *Family First*, and he invited me to participate in the Family Reunion Conference in Tennessee. I was on a panel talking family and what family means. I talked about the need for people to get more involved with their kids and not always put their careers first. I've been part of the Family Reunion Conference every year since then and I've seen how it has grown. People come from all over the world and everyone goes away completely energized by the discussions and the networking opportunities they've been given. Vice-President and Mrs. Gore are always there, contributing their support and their enormous enthusiasm.

If you have walked the walk, you can identify with people in need and I believe that both the Clintons and the Gores, in different ways, have experienced the struggles and the hard times that allow them to identify. If you don't have that hands-on experience, how can you know what it's like?

So I say to people in low-income areas, people who have careers, go vote! If you believe this economy has made a difference, if it has helped you, then show it at the ballot box. You have a voice only when you make it heard. Only then can you make a difference.

Two of my children attended the University of North Carolina at Chapel Hill and I've been on the board of the School of Social Work there for many years. I'm now deeply involved with the Jordan Institute for Families there. I work hand-in-hand with the director of the program, Dr. Nancy Dickerson, to promote research into the needs, concerns and priorities of families and to insure that our findings become public policy. Just recently, for example, we went to Capitol Hill to campaign for the implementation of a National Family Day, a day when working people could take the time off to celebrate family by being with their own families. Anyone can talk about family values, but how can we be certain that the programs important to families are actually put into place? Many people did not have families there for them when they were growing up and that's why it's so important for us to educate our teenagers to know what parenting really means. If the Republicans don't understand that, then how will we ever teach our young people how to make this country a wonderful place where everyone can survive and thrive?

We've heard about issues like education from both Mr. Gore and Mr. Bush — so how do we decide what is real? I think we have to look at what each of the candidates has done in the past; we have to build on our beliefs and their credentials. We have to make our decision based on what they've done over the years. And I believe Mr. Gore's record and his actions speak for themselves.

Parenting, like everything else, starts with the small things. Several years ago, Diane Sawyer did a piece on national television about how I taught all my kids, Michael included, how to clean, wash clothes, do dishes, vacuum and, generally, to take care of themselves. And they all learned. After that program aired, we got letters from children all over the country asking me why I had to say that on national television. They said their parents were now really on their case. Their response made me laugh, but that didn't change what I really think is important — if you start with the little things, you can then move on to the big things.

In July, 1993 my husband was murdered — shot while two young men were trying to steal his car. Before that, you could have told me anything, but

I never would have believed that could happen. It has changed the lives of our whole family forever. I've tried not to be bitter about those two young men, but I am very angry with their parents, who gave them no guidance. One of the two had just gotten out of jail and he thought the world owed him something. Why didn't he just take the car? Because he had a gun and shooting was easier. That's why I'm so convinced that we must have more control over who gets guns. We must make sure they can't be peddled through the back door to people like this. Gun control is more important today than it ever was and I believe the tragedy at Columbine has brought that realization home to people across the nation. We need to register guns and to know how they will be used. We need to have rules and regulations that everyone must abide by. Everyone is worried. I'm worried about my own grandchildren. And everyone — parents and non-parents alike — should be worried. Once more it comes down simply to this — we must protect our children.

My one fear has always been that I wouldn't teach all my kids the proper values, values that would allow them to succeed no matter what they chose to do with their lives, so that they would be happy, and able to help someone else along the way. And I'm proud to say that I think I've managed to do that. Michael's enormous success is just gravy, because all my children are good and successful at what they've chosen to do. James Ronald has had a career in the army for 25 years and he loves it. My oldest daughter, Deloris, works in real estate, even though I thought she'd go into fashion. Larry works in marketing, and my baby, Rosalind, is a poet and a singer. Every child is different, even in one family the children are all different from one another, and you need to treat them differently. I'm doing it all over again now with my own grandchildren. I'm trying to tell them things they'll remember later on, so that years from now, when something comes up, they'll stop and think, "Oh, yeah, my grandma used to say…"

I'm proud of what President Clinton and Vice-President Gore have done for this country. They've done their jobs! That's why I believe so strongly that Mr. Gore will pick of the torch of leadership and that he'll continue to improve upon the programs this administration has put into place. It's more important than ever that everyone vote and that we vote to continue the policies of this Democratic administration. If you don't vote, you can't complain — you can't complain when there's a cut in the Medicare or Social Security budget, or in some other government program that directly affects your own family. So I say, vote for the children. Be sure *they* will have a voice! We have to believe in someone and I believe that everyone should have felt some results from what this administration has done for our country and for our economy. If you want that to continue, the ball is in your court!

———

Deloris Jordan

Mom…

Mrs. Jordan began her career long before her crowning titles as: mom of the famous Michael Jordan, public speaker, author and businesswoman; her pursuit and passion was to put excellence into her children. Moreover the mission of this great woman was to raise a family with values (treasures) that no one could vandalize or corrupt. Mr. and Mrs. Jordan deposited a wealth of love into the souls of their children. Therefore regardless of external and internal conflicts, the Jordan children would be anchored by unconditional love in an ever-changing world. Mrs. Jordan has maintained balance and stability in her life because of her Christian foundation.

The Jordan family: James, Delois, Larry, Michael and Roslyn.

Author…

The voice of motherhood, wit and wisdom, Mrs. Jordan is the author of two books "Family First" released in April 1996, highlighting the Seven Principles of Parenting and "Salt In his Shoes" published by Simon & Schuster, scheduled for release in November 2000. Her daughter Roslyn Jordan is the co-author of the children's book "Salt In His Shoes" which tells a story of Michael Jordan in pursuit of a dream. Mrs. Jordan has also contributed a chapter to the book "I Will Follow Christ" with J. Countryman, published by Word Publishing due to be released September 2000.

Business Woman/Entrepreneur...

Mrs. Jordan began her working career at Corning Glass Works and United Carolina Bank, Wilmington, N.C. However, Michael's success on the basketball court gave way to an exciting new path and career; soon Deloris Jordan would make an impact on the world. Her extraordinary warmth, intelligence, quiet confidence and mother voice shined in the media. "Who was the mother behind this king who reigned on the basketball court?" Mrs. Jordan was propelled into her destiny.

She was the President and Co-Founder of the Michael Jordan Foundation, which opened its doors in September of 1989. Through the MJ Foundation Mrs. Jordan has been able to give $6 million to needy organizations over the last several years. With the closing of the MJ Foundation, a great portion of her efforts have been directed towards the James Jordan Boys & Girls Club and Family Life Center, which opened its doors in September 1997 on the West Side of Chicago, to aid many underprivileged and disadvantaged youths and their families. Additionally, Mrs. Jordan is the President and Founder of the James R. Jordan Foundation and De'Laro, Inc.

An advocate for children and family, Mrs. Jordan has worked with the Children's Defense Fund and its founder Marian Wright-Elderman, S.C. Johnson (a family business) on their Inhalant Abuse Program in Wisconsin and Christian Family Care Agency in Phoenix, Ariz. She has also worked with Mountain Ridge Community Church in Seattle, Wash., Family Re-union at Vanderbilt University in Tennessee and was a panelist along with Vice-President Al Gore discussing "What do families want in their communities?" an annual conference that she has attended over the last four years.

Board Affiliations...

Mrs. Jordan currently serves on several Boards: LaRabida, Children's Hospital and Research Center, The Jordan Family Institute, Audrey Hepburn Hollywood for Children Foundation, Foundation for Peace & Stability in Liberia, School of Social Work, University of North Carolina at Chapel Hill, Jordan Universal Marketing Products, Inc. (J.U.MP.) and the James Jordan Boys and Girls Club & Family Life Center/Honorary Chair

Awards and Honors...

Mrs. Jordan has received many awards for her outstanding service to improve the lives of others. Included among them are: Unicef Award presented by Audrey Hepburn,

Honored in 1997 as one of 100 Women Making A Difference along with former Illinois first lady Brenda Edgar, 1998 Black Trumpet Award presented by Ted Turner, Humanitas Award/St. Colleta's of Illinois, Mary Potter Humanitarian Award/Little Company of Mary Hospital, Family Resilience Award/ The Chicago Center for Family Health of the University of Chicago, 1999 Outstanding Mother of the Year Award/National-New York, 1999 Mother of the Year Award/Jack and Jill Foundation (South Suburban Chapter) and the 1999 Raoul Wallenberg Humanitarian Award/Shaare Zedek Medical Center.

CHAPTER EIGHT

★

JOSEPH
LIEBERMAN

ON POLITICS AS A CAREER

*T*here are times, now and then, when my mother will read something critical about me in the newspapers, or she'll hear the fatigue in my voice during an evening phone conversation from my home in Washington to hers in Connecticut. "Sweetheart," she'll say in that voice I've heard all my life, "do you really need this?"

I laugh and answer, "Yes, Mom, I really do need this. I love it."

Of course, my mother knows what my answer will be, and I know she is proud of it. But her question makes a good point. There's a lot you have to learn to live with if you are going to hold elected office and live a public life in America today. Privacy, for example, is difficult to maintain, for you and your family. Criticism, when you receive it (and you can count on receiving it, from political adversaries, if not from the man on the street or from the media), is sometimes searing, frequently personal and almost always public.

The media — newspapers, television, radio — shadow public officials' every move, analyzing their words and deeds, scrutinizing their intentions, second-guessing their decisions and questioning their intelligence, not to mention their integrity. In this age of around-the-clock live cable television news, radio and Internet, those judgements are instantly and constantly transmitted, day in and day out, to tens of millions of viewers, listeners and readers, often without adhering to the traditional journalistic standards of accuracy and reliability.

It's hard to imagine a career — other than professional athletics or entertainment — where one's job performance is as visible, as studied and as magnified as a politician's. Like an athlete and an entertainer, an elected official today must face questions not only about how he is doing his job but how he is living his life — and how he had lived his life. Besides being expected to account for almost any aspect of his present existence, he may be asked to explain things he did years or even decades ago, long before he entered public life. Unlike an athlete and an entertainer, whose wayward behavior — past or present — can often embellish a career, a politician's words and deeds are typically held to the highest of standards, and he is, in the most acutely direct sense, answerable for those actions — answerable to the public. They are the people who hired him. They are the people who can fire him. And they are also the people to whom he must constantly turn for not only approval but also tangible support.

If you are going to live the life of a politician, you have to learn to ask people for support — political and financial. That is not always easy or comfortable. You have to ask them as well for their votes. And you have to be aware that they might want something in return that you may not be able to give them, which they may not understand, and which they may therefore resent.

As a politician, you will also have to endure the disdain of those who consider your profession little more than bartering political favors for money and votes. You may well be sullied by the fight for election, drawn into the kind of negative campaigning and mudslinging that leaves both winners and losers dirtied and degraded in the public eye. Upon entering office, you will step into yet another arena that has turned uglier than ever before, this one infected with the partisan infighting of political parties that are polarized today to a degree unequaled in our nation's recent history.

So why in the world would anyone in his or her right mind choose such a life?

Well, I'm afraid fewer and fewer people are choosing it. This is bad for our democracy.

I had lunch not long ago with a group of interns in my Senate office. I try to do this each summer, at the end of these students' time with us, as a way of thanking them and saying goodbye before they head back to their colleges. This particular group came from a broad mix of campuses, including UCLA, the University of Virginia, Trinity College, the College of William and Mary and my alma mater, Yale. Toward the end of the meal, I asked how many of them were thinking about pursuing a career in public life after graduation. Most were, which was not surprising. They probably wouldn't have spent their summer on Capitol Hill if they weren't. But when I went further and asked how many of their friends and classmates were considering a career in politics, they said not many, if any. I asked why.

"They think," said one, "that politics is just a lot of noise and not much is accomplished."

"It's too partisan," said another. "And too nasty. And politicians don't have any privacy."

"Too often," said a third, "it seems like politicians spend most of their time raising money — big money."

Meanness. Big money. Partisanship.

Not much accomplished.

The reasons these students ticked off for their classmates' aversion mirror the disdain most of the nation feels right now for politics and for politicians.

That is not suprising when you think about the sordid spectacle that culminated in the impeachment trail of President Bill Clinton, the partisan bickering and bloodletting unleashed throughout that national crisis, the aura of zealous pursuit infecting the independent counsel's investigation, the media's seemingly unquenchable thirst for scandal, the ascent of a character like Larry Flynt as a moral arbiter and influence on this monumental process. In the wake of such a gaudy and demeaning saga at what is supposed to be the highest, most dignified level of our society, is it any wonder that Americans by the millions simply turned away in disappointment and disgust?

Voter turnout for the November 1998 elections, which followed the President's nationally televised "confession" of his relationship with Monica Lewinsky and the subsequent beginning of the impeachment proceedings in the House, was 36 percent — the lowest for any midterm election since 1942. Think about that number. For every eligible American who voted, there were two who did not.

The disheartening statistic tells us that fewer Americans than ever can muster enough trust in their government to conclude that it is worth voting. This cynicism has infected the American people to the point where a disturbingly large number of them no longer believe that public life in our democracy — the very core of our system of representative government — is worthy of their respect, let alone their involvement. In a survey taken in 1964, three out of four Americans said they believed in their government and trusted their elected leaders. A similar survey taken last year found that figure had dropped to one in four.

One in four.

Public confidence did not plummet overnight. It did not begin with Bill Clinton. Politicians and government have endured suspicion and a certain degree of scorn since the birth of this nation. This skepticism on the part of the American public is a grand tradition, as deeply rooted in our society as the spirit of freedom and independence and limited government. What is new, however, is the degree to which that suspicion and scorn have grown in the past 30 years. These three decades have seen an unprecedented parade of betrayals of the public's trust, from the deception that lay behind the Vietnam War, to the shock of the Watergate scandal, to Iran-Contra and the partisan political and cultural warfare that erupted in the 1980's, to the personal attacks on public figures such as Judge Robert Bork, Speaker Jim Wright and Justice Clarence Thomas, to the unseemly revelations of campaign finance wrongdoing in 1996 and on through the earthshaking impeachment experience of 1998 and 1999.

That's an awful beating for a political system to take over the course of just one generation. And it has brought us to a low point in the American people's relationship with their government. They are experiencing a real crisis of confidence not just in politicians but in the value of public life in our democracy, which troubles me deeply because I've lived that life for those same 30 years — virtually my entire adulthood — and I think it deserves better. I've experienced its challenges and satisfactions and I've felt its pitfalls and pressures. I know the strains it can put on a personal life — on a marriage and a family. I've felt the probing eye of the media push further and further into public officials' offices and homes. I've seen the role of money in political campaigns grow more uncontrollable and corrosive year after year. I've felt the viciousness of partisanship infect the process of politics to the point where reasonable collaboration becomes almost impossible. I've watched good men go bad, their judgement clouded by zealotry and ideological obligation, by egos and ambition, by the dark side of power and prestige, or simply and sadly by desires that become needs.

The American people have watched these things as well. Every day, on the pages of hundreds of newspapers and magazines, they read ringside accounts of the latest political battle, or corruption, or scandal. Every day they watch the constant flow of television news broadcasts. They listen to analysts on radio talk shows dissect and diagnose the political news of the day with each other, with the audience and with the politicians themselves. They scour the Internet. And for a firsthand look at government doing its business, they watch C-SPAN.

With such a wealth of access and input, it's easy to feel that we've got more than enough information about public life and those who are living it to make conclusive judgements about the quality, the value and even the future of that life.

But, with all that Americans are shown of public life through the media, there is more that they do not see that is good and hopeful. There are aspects of life in government that are not conveyed by today's cameras and tape recorders that are fascinating, encouraging and even enjoyable. Without understanding these fuller dimensions of this life, it is hard to honestly and accurately judge it, or to prescribe solutions for what ails it. Communicating that more complete picture of public life is exactly what I want to do.

Last year a group called the Council for Excellence in Government sponsored a poll that found that two out of three Americans feel "disconnected" from their government, that more than half our society does not believe the government is any longer "of, by and for the people," and that the segment of society that feels most estranged from government is the young, ages 18 to 34.

This is what those interns were trying to tell me at lunch and this is what chills me most — the prospect of the best of the next generation turning their backs on politics and public life. It is always, of course, the young upon whom the future direction of our society depends and right now that generation is abandoning its government.

Not that they don't care about society. In fact, while those who are now coming of age in America may feel disconnected from government, they do feel a strong connection to their community and its needs, stronger in some ways than the generations that preceded them in the 1970s and 1980s. While they may be shunning political careers, they are turning in growing numbers toward public service — community groups, advocacy groups — and volunteer work. A recent national study of college freshmen shows that more students are choosing schoolteaching as a career than at any time in the past quarter century. Why? Certainly not for ego or pay. No, the reason cited repeatedly by the students in this survey was their desire to "make a difference."

Of course, we should celebrate the fact that these young people are choosing to turn talent, vision and hope not toward just themselves — as seemed to be prevalent in the '80s — but toward one another, toward their community, toward those in need.

But it also brings me back to the question I asked at the beginning: Why in the world would anyone, including the next generation, choose to live the public life of a politician today? Why, to repeat my mother's question, do I really need this?

The answer, I would suggest, is the same one those future teachers gave: to make a difference. For all that is wrong with our system of government, and there is much that needs repair, it remains a place where one can truly and uniquely make a difference, where one can help improve our country and even occasionally, the world.

We need to convince more young people who want to make a difference to enter public life. For the American experiment in self-government to remain vital, we need more people to serve that government and to live public lives. If we didn't have politicians, we would have to invent them. We can turn our backs and abandon them in disgust, thereby ensuring that the government does indeed belong to the privileged and powerful few. Or we can conclude that public life is a worthy pursuit, that it can be an honorable, constructive, satisfying, enjoyable career, deserving of the best among us.

We need to nurture this belief, especially in the generation now coming of age. We need to restore the trust and faith that have been so badly damaged. If this sounds as if I'm talking about a personal or even a marital relationship it should. Trust is the foundation of any relationship, and the first step toward repairing the people's damaged trust in their government is to establish a foundation of clarity, honesty and understanding.

It is toward that end that I want to share some of what I've come to know and understand about public life over the course of my own career.

I'm still living that life, still learning, still trying to figure out how to deal with and repair the problems that persist. I will also describe what I believe is right and good about this life, which, in my opinion, far outweighs the bad. I write in praise of public life for all who care about the future of our democracy.

In 1976, in the wake of the Watergate scandal, Jimmy Carter came up with a wonderful one-line insight about the relationship between the public and its elected leadership: The American people, he said, deserve a government as good as they are.

Nearly a quarter century later, the American people still deserve as much and they still do not have it. But my life in politics tells me they are closer to it than they think.

There is much talk these days of the "rampant careerism" that has, in the view of some observers, come to infect our government. The term "professional politician" is pronounced with distaste, the implication being that holding public office cannot be both a calling and a career, that the later inevitably contaminates the former. Government, from this point of view, has become a wasteful haven for men and women with suspect motives who settle into its recesses for the duration, feeding from the public trough, fattening themselves on power and influence while constantly raising money for reelection and only fitfully producing anything of substance.

The solution? Do away with the "Beltway insiders." Replace them, as Ross Perot once suggested, with "citizen amateurs." Impose term limits to make sure no one hangs around too long.

This scorn of political "careerists" is nothing new. When our nation was created, the Founding Fathers felt strongly that those who hold elected office should do it as a public service, not as a profession, and should rotate in and out of public office after a limited period of time. The men who agreed to govern (they were all men then) had well-established successful non-legislative careers — farming, shipping, commerce — to which they returned once their time in office was over. George Washington, Thomas Jefferson, James Madison, were "gentlemen" of the upper class drafted by their colleagues and contemporaries to offer their skills and services to their fledgling country. They saw themselves as public servants, virtually as volunteers. Although they spent much of their lives in service of their country, it was considered unseemly to actively seek office, and unthinkable to consider public life your "job."

But it is important to understand that term limits, which were a feature of the Articles of Confederation, were not included in the Constitution because they didn't work. They had hobbled the performance of our pre-Constitutional government. Term-limited, part-time lawmakers and governors at the federal and state levels were either weak or absent. They literally failed to show up for work because they were busy elsewhere. By the turn of the 19th century, government began to attract a different breed of officeholder, politicians who actively pursued seats in Congress and, once they had them, made it clear that they intended to stay. That brought an entirely different set of risks and advantages. The Senate, with its six-year terms, its relatively small membership and the prospect of these members' perpetual reelection, became a particular worrisome place to some. Henry Clay, writing to his wife in the 1830's, complained that the Senate was "no longer a place for any decent man. It is rapidly filling up with blackguards."

Those sentiments are prevalent today — about the Senate, the House and even the presidency. I don't disagree that there are, and always have been, legitimate concerns in our society about the character and motivation of the people who choose politics as a career, since we are, after all, human. But to suspect those who make it their career, simply because they have made it their career, to pronounce them "professionals" as if that were a derogatory term, demeans the important work our society needs professional politicians to do.

To call someone a professional implies that he or she has attained a high level of expertise at what he or she does. We generally respect that. We value it. When we need a plumber, we seek a professional. The same is true with a neurologist, or an architect, or a hairstylist. Why should we ask any less of the people who run our government?

In most cases, in most professions, expertise comes from experience. It is built over time. It is typically attained by working with and learning from other professionals in the same field. This is as true of government as it is of carpentry. What I learned about the complexities of legislation during the 10 years I spent as a state senator in Connecticut was invaluable when I became a United State senator. And what I have learned during my 11 years on Capital Hill makes me a much better senator today than I was when I began.

Of course I'm not saying that our political system should not sometimes be shaken up through the election of a new kind of leader, such as Jesse Ventura in our time, or that it should not be open to the fresh perspective of someone from an entirely different profession, a person who has been successful, say, in business, or, as in the case of one of my Senate colleagues, Bill Frist of Tennessee, in medicine. But we would not want to have a Senate composed of 100 people who had never held public office before. It would not govern well.

Remember, our advanced society operates on the concept of division of labor. The entirely self-sufficient individual in America today is nearly nonexistent. Few of us have the skills needed to raise our own food, build our own houses or mend our own wounds. We are each more or less specialists, experts to one degree or another at what we do, dependent upon other specialists to do what they do to take care of our needs. There is, built into this system, a great degree of freedom and comfort. We can rest assured that while we are doing our job, others are doing theirs. The police, for instance. And food inspectors. Air traffic controllers. And, yes, politicians. A friend of mine who is not in government, informing me recently that she was going to the ballet that evening, put it this way: "You're taking care of the government tonight so I don't have to."

That's why the notion of term limits has never made sense to me. It precludes the possibility of a legislator building expertise over time. It denies the value of experience. And it ignores the fact that our political system already includes built-in term limits decided by the voting public every two, or four, or six years — they are called elections.

Where the concept of political careerism truly becomes an issue, it seems to me, is around the question of purpose. It is important, of course, to understand a person's purpose for choosing to enter political life. In almost every case I know of, as a person begins his political career, those intentions are honorable and sincere. But they don't always stay that way. Once people enter this life, they become vulnerable to a host of pressures and forces that can skew their purposes, sometimes without their awareness. It is these forces — partisanship, special interest groups, the need for money, the demands of campaigning, the power of the media — that can twist a politician's priorities and make keeping one's seat become more important than what one does while sitting in it. That is when the voters should, and usually do, vote the wayward politician out of office, because that's the way the system cleanses and corrects itself.

———————

JOSEPH LIEBERMAN

Joseph Lieberman was born in Stamford, Conn. on Feb. 24, 1942 and attended public schools there. He received his bachelor's degree from Yale College in 1964 and his law degree from Yale Law School in 1967.

Lieberman was elected to the Connecticut State Senate in 1970 and served there for 10 years, including the last six as Majority Leader. He also spent time in the private practice of law and as an Assistant Dean of the School of Art and Architecture at Yale.

He is the author of five books. The most recent, "In Praise of Public Life" (2000), is a spirited defense of public life that draws on his personal experience.

From 1982 to 1988, Joe Lieberman served as Connecticut's 21st Attorney General, and used the post to fight for consumers in Connecticut. He won a multi-million dollar case against supermarket chains and even took on a powerful insurance company from his home state. He took on the oil industry and brought legal actions to promote women's rights. Lieberman also was an aggressive enforcer of the state's environmental protection laws.

In 1988, Lieberman won the biggest upset victory in the country, by beating incumbent Lowell Weicker to win election to the U.S. Senate by just 10,000 votes. Six years later, he made history by winning the biggest landslide victory ever in a Connecticut race for a Senate seat, with a margin of more than 67 percent of the vote.

Now in his second term in the U. S. Senate, Joe Lieberman has earned a national reputation as a thoughtful, effective legislator. He is a Democrat who speaks his conscience, forms bipartisan coalitions with Republicans and fights for working families. He has fought for consumers, for a better environment for present and future generations and for a strong national defense in his service in the Senate and on the Armed Services, Environment and Public Works, Governmental Affairs, and Small Business Committees.

In endorsing his reelection in 1994, the New York Times wrote, "Congress would be a better place if more of his veteran colleagues were as good. In only one term he has influenced the course of Federal legislation for the benefit of Connecticut and the nation." Countless commentators have recognized Lieberman as a voice of conscience, integrity, ethics and moderation in the Senate.

Lieberman, who is Jewish, lives in New Haven with his wife Hadassah. They are the parents of four children: Matthew, Rebecca, Ethan and Hana. He also has two granddaughters, Tennessee and Willie.

CHAPTER NINE

★

MARC POLLICK

GIVING BACK:
THE PUBLIC-PRIVATE PARTNERSHIP

*T*here is a moral imperative in politics and it has nothing to do with the personal morality of officeholders. Its roots can be traced back to the first Passover Seder, which Jews celebrated to commemorate the Exodus from Egypt. While the central theme of the Seder is freedom, a precursor and necessary ingredient of democracy, freedom from bondage is but one of the freedoms illumined in the story. Also critical to political freedom is "freedom from hunger." In fact, a Seder cannot begin before the master of the house opens the front door and proclaims "let all who are hungry come and eat." The lesson is symbolically and dramatically imparted to all present that no one can truly enjoy political freedom without also enjoying freedom from want.

Simply put, a society is judged by how it treats its most dispossessed citizens. Helping those less fortunate is a public-private compact between a government that understands and accepts that responsibility and a citizenry who cares enough to do its share to give back. Anyone that has ever watched two children play in a sandbox knows that "giving" and "sharing one's wealth" is not innate in human beings. It is a value that must be taught. This is no less true on a national level.

Franklin D. Roosevelt, in his second inaugural address, framed the challenge for all Americans when he proclaimed, "The test of our progress is not whether we add more to the abundance of those who have much; it is whether we provide enough for those who have too little." Expanding upon that same sentiment and placing it within a moral context was Hubert H. Humphrey who said, "The moral test of government is how it treats those who are in the dawn of life, the children; those who are in the twilight of life, the elderly; and those in the shadows of life, the sick, the needy and the handicapped." Throughout the history of our Republic, one party has taken unto itself this moral and civic imperative that we are all collectively responsible for our neighbors; that there is a public-private partnership between philanthropy and government programs that takes cognizance of the most vulnerable among us. Such a partnership lends credence to the supposition that a community — indeed a country — can only be as strong as its weakest link. That party is the party of FDR and Hubert Humphrey.

The Democratic Party has always understood that the so-called "safety net," so callously dismantled by the Reagan Administration during the 1980's, is as much a bulwark for the health of our country as it is a lifeline for our fellow citizens who fall between the cracks. Community building and the concept of giving back have been central tenets of the Clinton-Gore Administration, as exemplified by bold and innovative programs like Americorps, the President's One America Initiative and the Initiative on Race. The very well-being of a democracy is based in large part on the involvement of its citizens in institution building and volunteerism. The energy of the past eight years — years of unparalleled wealth creation in this nation — has been an energy augmented by the unwavering belief that charitable giving and volunteerism are two principal pillars of a healthy democracy.

In my role as President and founder of The Giving Back Fund, I was privileged to attend the very first White House Conference on Philanthropy: Gifts to the Future. The Conference was convened by The First Lady and President Clinton in October, 1999 as a result of years of discussion about the need to focus the nation's attention on the importance of honoring, sustaining and expanding the unique American tradition of giving. The conference emphasized that at this moment of great prosperity, we must preserve and indeed, expand this tradition. During his remarks, The President noted that the national average for per capita charitable giving is just 2 percent of gross income (we are hardly a nation of tithers!). By simply raising charitable giving a mere 1 percent, to 3 percent of gross income, we would be able to fund untold numbers of important social programs that would have a profound impact on children, the elderly and the handicapped in our country.

Directly in line with the Conference's call to expand and sustain philanthropy, The Giving Back Fund is a 3- year-old national nonprofit organization that actively promotes, encourages and facilitates new and diverse philanthropy, targeting especially professional athletes and entertainers. This group, largely celebrities, is comprised of a disproportionately high percentage of African-Americans and Hispanics, youth and women – welcome and important additions to the philanthropic arena. Hoping to combine celebrity and wealth, and leverage both on behalf of philanthropy, I brought with me to the conference an 18-year-old teen idol named Justin Timberlake from the sensationally popular musical group 'NSYNC.

Justin had determined just a few weeks earlier to create a charitable foundation with The Giving Back Fund to support music programs in America's public schools. I felt the conference would provide the perfect forum for Justin to announce his new foundation. One compelling reason the First Lady said she had convened the conference was to call for more role models in philanthropy. Here was a young man, still in his teens, a superstar performer and already fabulously wealthy, who genuinely cared about "giving back." Not only did he care; he wanted to act on that caring. That day at the White House he was the only speaker to speak entirely without notes. Before the President and the First Lady, and some of the most illustrious philanthropists in America, Justin Timberlake spoke from the heart about what moved him to want to give back and, in so doing, established himself as an eloquent and powerful role model for philanthropy.

Largely inspired by that conference, The Giving Back Fund is creating the nation's Philanthropy Hall of Fame to annually enshrine one or more individuals who have promoted philanthropy selflessly throughout the course of his or her lifetime. Also recognized and honored each year will be extraordinary acts of generosity and philanthropic deeds across a wide variety of categories including volunteerism, corporate philanthropy, anonymous giving, per capita giving, philanthropy by children under the age of 16, community giving, etc. We are a generous country and we should take note of and celebrate all the manifestations of that generosity. Nothing could be more rewarding, or more enriching for our nation, than for all Americans to acquire the habit of giving.

It was no coincidence that this President and this First Lady convened the first White House Conference on Philanthropy. For they came of age and formed important values about the role of an engaged and active citizenry about the same time that John F. Kennedy exhorted all Americans to "Ask not, what your country can do for you, instead, ask what you can do for your country."

In a letter to conference participants, Vice-President Al Gore wrote, "I became involved in public service because I believe strongly that one person can make a positive difference for others. As you and your organizations have demonstrated, citizens from all walks of life can work together to claim our nation's challenges as their own, building bridges among people and setting powerful examples of leadership and compassion. In partnership (there's that word again) with government, schools, and religious communities, caring individuals and groups are expanding and encouraging the great American legacy of philanthropy and I am proud to recognize each of you for the work you are doing for your community and our country."

"Powerful examples of leadership and compassion…" For Al Gore, compassion is not a mere adjective, employed to modify or make more palatable a not very compassionate political philosophy. What Al Gore understands is that compassion requires action. For him, and for the President he serves, it is a central core value affecting all for which they have so steadfastly stood. Running a compassionate administration requires more than lip service to the vexing problems of our nation concerning poverty, race relations, equal opportunity, universal access to health care, and adequate attention to citizens with special needs. It requires government working in concert with the private sector, in an honest and active attempt to alleviate suffering and injustice. If that necessitates bigger government, than it does. It will also invariably necessitate more philanthropy, more volunteerism and more federal programs like the Corporation for National Service, which promotes youth initiatives.

President Clinton took an important step in this direction recently when he ordered the creation of an Interagency Task Force on Nonprofits and Government to examine the federal government's relationship with the voluntary sector. The new effort is designed to improve the service provided by government agencies to nonprofit organizations. Bold leaders routinely take such initiatives because they know in their bones that if the American people cannot depend on their own government for compassion, to whom can they turn? Such leaders are rewarded for their vision and understanding by the respect of their countrymen and the continuation of their jobs.

We have enormous opportunity before us. The historic rise in personal wealth created over the past eight years has provided historic opportunities in philanthropy. These opportunities can best be maximized by a full partner on the side of government if we are to meet the great challenges before us. Educational opportunity is still not afforded all children in our country equally (read Jonathan Kozol, Savage Inequalities, Rachel and Her Children, Amazing Grace). Health care is still not available to all our citizens. We cannot trust these moral imperatives to a government that believes wealth should flow to the few on top and hopefully, maybe, "trickle down" to those less fortunate below. If we allowed those policies to prevail, we would fail FDR's test of progress and Hubert Humphrey's moral test of government. Our fellow citizens are depending on us to seize this opportunity. We cannot afford to fail them, for if we do, we will be failing ourselves as well.

While personal income has risen to meteoric heights over these last few years, the gap between the very rich and the middle class has also increased significantly. We risk the danger of becoming a country of "haves" and "have-nots". Our nation stands on the precipice of an intergenerational wealth transfer unprecedented in human history. Estimates range into the double figure trillions of dollars. With the prospects of this wealth transfer so rife with possibility, it behooves us to ask, "what kind of nation do we want to have?" Now is no time to be conservative about our compassion. True compassion requires bold initiatives, active engagement and cold cash. It is one matter to create new wealth and steward a prosperous economy. It is yet another challenge to employ wealth responsibly and to expand generosity through carefully targeted giving opportunities.

To expand philanthropy, government must protect philanthropy. As a nation, we can redistribute wealth in powerful and creative ways through charitable giving. To do this our leaders must nurture and encourage a culture of giving back. The Clinton-Gore Administration has done that by calling for new role models in philanthropy, by convening the White House Conference on Philanthropy and by standing firm against repealing the estate tax, which would surely result in a severe decline in charitable giving through the elimination of the tax incentive to make charitable bequests. This President has chosen instead to be proactive with regard to promoting philanthropy through the proposal of an entire package of new tax incentives aimed at encouraging greater charitable giving.

A strong economy usually indicates strong and capable leadership in Washington. Compassionate leadership recognizes that not everyone can prosper at the same time and those who cannot are no less our fellow citizens and no less our collective responsibility. Those kind of leaders, the kind spoken of by FDR and Humphrey, view government and private sector philanthropy as lifelong partners in the quest for a just society.

Will we pass the test of progress and the moral test of government? As the richest nation on earth, will we provide enough for those who have too little? Will we treat with dignity and respect, those in the dawn, the twilight and the shadows of life? How we choose our leaders as we enter this new millennium will answer those questions and will have a profound effect on the kind of society, and nation, we live in.

MARC POLLICK

Marc Pollick is President, CEO, and founder of The Giving Back Fund, a national non-profit organization that helps athletes, entertainers, and other create and manage charitable entities. Founded in 1997, The Giving Back Fund is comprised of many individually identified donor-advised foundations each with its own independent philanthropic interests and initiatives. Inspired by a speech by Hillary Rodham Clinton during the 1999 White House Conference on Philanthropy, Pollick is creating the nation's Philanthropy Hall of Fame, which will honor philanthropy in all its aspects, whether manifested by the giving of time, talent or money.

Before founding The Giving Back Fund, Marc Pollick was a consultant for the Elie Wiesel Foundation for Humanity and the founder of its predecessor, The Elie Wiesel Institute for Humanitarian Studies. Pollick also served as the Assistant Director of the Center for Jewish Studies at Harvard University.

After graduating from the University of Chicago in 1975, Mr. Pollick earned graduate degrees in Social Science, East European Jewish History and Holocaust Studies. He pursued his doctoral studies at Boston University under the direction of Professor Elie Wiesel, winner of the 1986 Nobel Prize for Peace. He lectures often throughout the United States and Israel and has taught courses on The Holocaust at the high school and university levels.

In 1982, Pollick was appointed Founding Executive Director of the Zachor Institute for Holocaust Studies in Miami, Fla. One year later, he created and hosted the cable TV series, We Remember. He has twice led student groups to Holocaust sites in Eastern Europe and, in 1983, led the first-ever group of children of Holocaust survivors on a Journey of Conscience to Eastern Europe and Israel. In 1989, he served as a senior researcher for the permanent exhibition of the United States Holocaust Memorial Museum.

Pollick nurtured his life-long love of sports playing basketball and track and field at the University of Chicago, where he won four varsity "Major C" athletic awards. He lives with his wife and two young children in Wellesley, Mass.

CHAPTER TEN

★

CHRISTOPHER REEVE

THE 2000 ELECTION AND BIOMEDICAL RESEARCH

*O*ver the last few years, we've heard a lot about something called family values. And like many of you, I've struggled to figure out what that means. But since my accident, I've found a definition that seems to make sense. I think it means that we're all family, that we all have value. And if that's true, if America really is a family, then we have to recognize that many members of our family are hurting.

Just to take one aspect of it, one in five of us have some kind of disability. You may have an aunt with Parkinson's disease. A neighbor with a spinal cord injury. A brother with AIDS. And if we're really committed to this idea of family we have got to do something about it.

First of all, our nation cannot tolerate discrimination of any kind. That's why the Americans with Disabilities Act is so important and must be honored everywhere. It is a civil rights law that is tearing down barriers both in architecture and in attitude.

Its purpose is to give the disabled access not only to buildings but to every opportunity in society. I strongly believe our nation must give its full support to the caregivers who are helping people with disabilities live independent lives.

Sure, we have got to balance the budget. And we will.

We have to be extremely careful with every dollar that we spend. But we also have got to take care of our family — and not slash programs people need. We should be enabling, healing, curing.

One of the smartest things we can do about disability is invest in research that will protect us from disease and lead to cures. This country already has a long history of doing just that. When we put our minds to a problem, we can usually find solutions. But our scientists can do more. And we have got to give them the chance.

That means more funding for research. Right now, for example, about 250,000 Americans have a spinal cord injury. Our government spends about $8.7 billion a year just maintaining these members of our family. But we spend only $40 million a year on research that would actually improve the quality of their lives, get them off public assistance and even cure them.

We have got to be smarter, do better. Because the money we invest in research today is going to determine the quality of life of members of our family tomorrow.

During my rehabilitation, I met a young man named Gregory Patterson. When he was innocently driving through Newark, N.J., a stray bullet from a gang shooting went through his car window…right into his neck and severed his spinal cord. Five years ago, he might have died. Today, because of research, he's alive.

But merely being alive is not enough. We have a moral and economic responsibility to ease his suffering and prevent others from experiencing such pain. And to do that we don't need to raise taxes. We just need to raise our expectations.

America has a tradition many nations probably envy: we frequently achieve the impossible. That's part of our national character. That's what got us from one coast to another. That's what got us the largest economy in the world. That's what got us to the moon.

On the wall of my room when I was in rehab was a picture of the space shuttle blasting off, autographed by every astronaut now at NASA. On the top of the picture it says, "We found nothing is impossible." That should be our motto. Not a Democratic motto, not a Republican motto. But an American motto. Because this is not something one party can do alone. It's something that we as a nation must do together.

So many of our dreams at first seem impossible, then they seem improbable and then, when we summon the will, they soon become inevitable. If we can conquer outer space, we should be able to conquer inner space, too: the frontier of the brain, the central nervous system and all the afflictions of the body that destroy many lives and rob our country of so much potential.

Research can provide hope for people who suffer from Alzheimer's. We've already discovered the gene that causes it. Research can provide hope for people such as Muhammad Ali and the Rev. Billy Graham who suffer from Parkinson's. Research can provide hope for the millions of Americans such as Kirk Douglas who suffer from stroke. We can ease the pain of people such as Elizabeth Glaser, whom we lost to AIDS. And now that we know that nerves in the spinal cord can regenerate, we are on our way to getting millions of people around the world such as me up and out of our wheelchairs.

Fifty-six years ago, FDR dedicated new buildings for the National Institutes of Health. He said the "the defense this nation seeks involves a great deal more than building airplanes, ships, guns and bombs. We cannot be a strong nation unless we are a healthy nation." He could have said that today.

President Roosevelt showed us that a man who could barely lift himself out of a wheelchair could still lift a nation out of despair. And I believe – and so does this administration – in the most important principle FDR taught us: America does not let its needy citizens fend for themselves. America is stronger when all of us take care of all of us. Giving new life to that ideal is the challenge before us tonight.

Thank you very much.

The basis of my speech in 1996 was my strong conviction — shared by millions of Americans — that we are pragmatists more than philosophers. We have a long history of transforming visionary ideas into practical solutions. As Robert F. Kennedy said "I dream of things that never were and ask: 'Why not'?"

In the field of biomedical research, scientists have indeed taken us from the impossible to the improbable and now to the inevitable. Guided by the conviction that failure is not an option, researchers both at home and abroad have embraced the Democratic Party's principle that no one must be left behind.

The plea for more funding prompted an annual increase of 15 percent for the National Institutes of Health over the last four years. Hundreds of young PhDs and post-docs switched careers and joined the front lines in the battle against disorders of the brain and central nervous system. The term "incurable" has been banished from the medical vocabulary. We have mapped the human genome, discovered the virtually unlimited potential of both adult and embryonic stem cells, and developed new techniques for early intervention in the acute phase of illness and injury. It is fair to say that astonishing progress has been made in a very short period of time.

More importantly however, victims of rare diseases and disabilities are now being brought in from the margins of society, leading more productive lives and gaining the recognition they deserve as valuable members of the American family.

I believe that the first Presidential election of the new millennium is of great historical significance. We now have an unprecedented opportunity to relieve human suffering. In 1996 we made a promise to do our best to examine catastrophic illness and injuries to see if anything could be done. Now in the year 2000 we can say to millions who suffer from Parkinson's, MS, cancer, strokes, ALS, Alzheimer's, spinal cord injury and more: "With enough funding and a committed partnership between the government and the private sector, we will be able to change your life."

Already clinicians are using stem cells taken from the pancreas to cure Type 1 diabetes. Stem cells harvested from umbilical cords are being used to cure sickle cell anemia. Adult stem cells found in the bone marrow are successfully treating bone marrow cancer. Scientists have begun clinical trials in remylina-tion, which is the key to reversing the debilitating affects of MS and certain types of spinal cord injury. Experiments with macrophages, scavenger cells that clear away debris at the site of trauma are now being used to limit the damage in the acute phase of brain injury.

Most of the leading investigators around the world are partnering with foundations, venture capitalists, pharmaceutical companies and government, working out logistics and projecting a timetable for an extraordinary range of human trials. As one expert recently said to me, "We are no longer intimidated by anything."

It is an understatement to say that cutting-edge researchers, facing the medical equivalent of climbing Mt. Everest without oxygen, are extremely cautious both in their work and how they talk about it. Never before have they been so optimistic. This election year is a perfect opportunity to join them and initiate a grassroots movement of support.

———◆———

CHRISTOPHER REEVE

Actor, director and activist are just some of the words used to describe Christopher Reeve. From his first appearance at the Williamstown Theatre Festival at the age of 15, Reeve established a reputation as one of the country's leading actors. However, since his injury in an equestrian competition in May, 1995, Reeve has put a human face on spinal cord injury.

After graduating from Cornell University, Reeve followed his dreams of acting, studying at Juilliard under the legendary John Houseman. He debuted on Broadway with Katharine Hepburn in "A Matter of Gravity." Reeve has distinguished himself in a variety of stage, screen and television roles, a passion that continues today. Film credits include: "Superman" in 1978 and its subsequent sequels, "Deathtrap," "Somewhere in Time," "The Bostonians," "Street Smart," "Speechless," "Village of the Damned," "Above Suspicion" and the Oscar-nominated "The Remains of the Day." Stage credits include: "The Marriage of Figaro," "Fifth of July," "My Life," "Summer and

Smoke," "Love Letters" and "The Aspern Papers."

Reeve made his directorial debut with "In the Gloaming" on HBO in April, 1997. The film was met with rave reviews, was nominated for five Emmys and won six Cable Ace Awards, including Best Dramatic Special. Reeve's autobiography, "Still Me," was published by Random House in April, 1998 and spent 11 weeks on the New York Times Bestseller List. His recording of "Still Me" earned Reeve a Grammy for Best Spoken Word in February, 1999. In his first major role since becoming paralyzed, Reeve starred an updated version of the classic Hitchcock thriller "Rear Window," for which he was nominated for a Golden Globe Award and won the Screen Actors Guild Award for Best Actor in a Television Movie or Miniseries. He also served as Executive Producer of the film.

While continuing to pursue his career in the arts, Reeve also remains focused on raising awareness about the profound impact medical research can have on all of our lives as well as other issues that impact those living with disabilities.

Reeve has become a powerful spokesperson for people with disabilities and for the benefits of medical research. His sharp intelligence, wit and curiosity have enabled him to become an advocate for all who are affected by diseases of the brain and central nervous system.

Reeve joined the Board of Directors of the American Paralysis Association (APA) in November, 1995 and in May of the following year, he became its Chairman. In January, 1996 Reeve and his wife Dana started the Christopher Reeve Foundation (CRF), a nonprofit organization dedicated to fighting paralysis caused by spinal cord injuries.

On April 14, 1999, Reeve gave hope to the hundreds of thousands affected by spinal cord injury when he announced the merger of the APA and the CRF. Leveraging the strengths of both organizations, the newly formed Christopher Reeve Paralysis Foundation (CRPF) will remain committed to the same goals that the APA has pursued over the past 17 years and CRF has embraced since its inception: to raise funds for medical research leading to a cure for spinal cord injury paralysis. CRPF also supports programs that improve the quality of life for people with disabilities. Reeve serves as Chairman of the Board of CRPF. Other board appointments include Vice Chairman of the National Organization on Disability and World T.E.A.M. Sports.

Reeve recently has:

- Lobbied on behalf of the National Institutes of Health as part of a group called NIHx2 to double the NIH budget in five years. In part because of his work, the NIH was appropriated a 15 percent increase in *funding for fiscal 1999, translating to more than $2 billion, the largest single increase ever;*

- *Provided instrumental and crucial support for the passage of the New York State Spinal Cord Injury Research Bill (7287C), landmark legislation which will make available up to $8.5 million annually in funds collected from violations of the state's vehicle and traffic laws to be appropriated among the leading research facilities in New York;*

- *Testified before the House Appropriations Subcommittee on Labor, Health and Human Services, Education and Related Agencies on behalf of the National Fund for Health Research Act;*

- *Worked with Senators Jeffords and Rockefeller and Congresswoman Eshoo to raise lifetime caps on insurance policies from $1million to $10 million;*

- *Served as a member of the Executive Committee of "Funding First," an initiative for medical research in honor of Mary Woodard Lasker, begun by former Senator Mark Hatfield;*

- *Joined with Senator Robert G. Torricelli to introduce legislation to create a national brain and spinal cord injury registry;*

- *Worked with Senator Jeffords to help pass the 1999 Work Incentives Improvement Act (S-331) in the U.S. Senate, which allows people with disabilities to return to work and still receive disability benefits;*

- *Established a line of celebrity neckwear that is carried at more than 1,000 JCPenney department stores across the United States. A portion of the proceeds benefits CRPF; and*

- *Continues to work tirelessly to obtain increased funding from both the public and private sectors to cure Parkinson's, Alzheimer's, MS, ALS, stroke, as well as to repair the damaged spinal cord.*

Not only is Reeve raising our awareness about the importance of medical research and the challenges facing those with disabilities, Reeve also is raising awareness about the need for families to have adequate health and disability coverage. In 1997, Reeve joined with HealthExtras, the first company to develop and price health and disability products for direct purchase via the Internet. Reeve serves as company spokesman.

Reeve's community and political involvement pre-dates his spinal cord injury. Over the course of many years, he has served as a national spokesman on behalf of the arts, campaign finance reform and the environment. He served as Co-President of The

Creative Coalition from 1992-1994, and also was involved with Save the Children, Amnesty International, National Resources Defense Council, The Environmental Air Force and America's Watch. In 1987, he demonstrated in Santiago, Chile on behalf of 77 actors threatened with execution by the Pinochet regime. For this action, Reeve was given a special Obie Award in 1988 and the annual award from the Walter Briehl Human Rights Foundation.

In addition to these many roles, Reeve is the father of three children and husband to wife, Dana. An inspiration to many, Reeve maintains a rigorous speaking schedule, traveling across the country giving motivational talks to numerous groups, organizations and corporations.

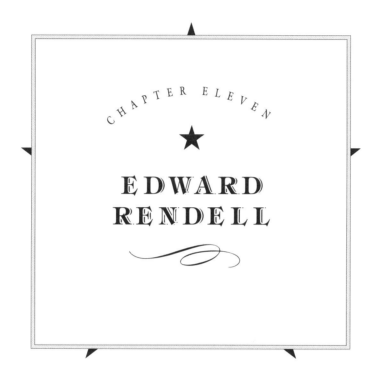

CHAPTER ELEVEN

EDWARD
RENDELL

I am sure that every good Democrat who attended the 2000 Democratic National Convention had his own political heroes. For some veterans of conventions, perhaps it's Franklin Roosevelt or Harry Truman. Many baby boomer democrats vividly remember the Camelot days of Jack and Bobby Kennedy. And for younger delegates, many of them came of age politically during the great campaign of 1992 that elected two fantastic Democrats? President Bill Clinton and Vice-President Al Gore.

My first political hero was my dad, Jesse Rendell. My father was a true blue Democrat who passed on to me his love of sports, his love of politics and especially the Democratic Party. He was a converter in the textile industry and only participated in politics as a voter. But he imbued in me his belief that government, especially government by Democrats, could make a difference in improving the quality of people's lives and that we had an obligation to make sure that government protected the most needy and vulnerable among us.

My dad died when I was very young, but I will forever remember one night in November 1952. We went down the street to pick up some groceries at the corner drug store and the radio was on behind the counter. As we approached it, the announcer relayed to us the tragic news — my dad's beloved Adlai Stevenson had gone down in defeat to Dwight David Eisenhower. It was the only time in my life that I can remember my dad crying.

Like many in his generation, my dad loved Stevenson. I guess you would call him today an unabashed liberal. And he thought that Adlai Stevenson was the embodiment of all those ideals.

My second political hero is a hero in the truest sense. In fact, in his career, he donned a cape and wore a big "S" on his chiseled chest. A generation of American kids looked up to Superman and thought there was nothing that could fell the legendary superhero (except of course kryptonite). As we all know, however, even Superman is susceptible to life's unkind twists and turns. A freak accident threw Christopher Reeve from his horse and paralyzed him from the neck down.

I know that many delegates to the 2000 Convention were with us in Chicago four years ago. Who among us can forget Christopher Reeve's moving address in the United Center? He said that Democrats, from FDR through the Clinton-Gore Administration, believed that the most important principle we have is that "America does not let its needy citizens fend for themselves. America is stronger when all of us take care of all of us."

When I heard those words from such a courageous person, shivers went down my spine. I thought of my dad and what he had taught me way back in 1952 and I was reminded once again, as clearly and as poignantly as ever, why I am a Democrat.

EDWARD RENDELL

Whether it's revitalizing the Democratic Party or the City of Philadelphia, Mayor Edward G. Rendell has a penchant for tackling enormous projects. As Mayor of Philadelphia, Ed Rendell led the comeback of a city once written off as "the city that sets the standard for municipal distress in the '90s." As General Chair of the Democratic National Committee, Ed Rendell will breathe new life into the Party as it prepares for the 2000 elections.

A native New Yorker, Ed Rendell arrived in Philadelphia in 1961 for his first year at the University of Pennsylvania. He served two terms as District Attorney and then ran for mayor on a platform that offered Philadelphia the hard truth about its future: To restore the city, to turn around decades of mismanagement and neglect, Philadelphians would have to join together in sacrifice and hard work and the shared belief that the politics of the past no longer provided the answers for the future. In January, 1992, Edward G. Rendell was inaugurated as Philadelphia's 121st mayor.

With the help of a determined City Council, Mayor Rendell erased Philadelphia's $230 million deficit, balanced the city's budget, and produced the first of what would become six straight budget surpluses, the last four of which have been the largest budget surpluses in the modern history of Philadelphia. Moreover, city services improved dramatically as the Rendell Administration plowed tax savings and greater productivity into on-time tax collection, six-day library services, and functioning public swimming pools and recreation centers.

Its fiscal house in order, Mayor Rendell led the charge to position Philadelphia as a premiere destination city to the point where Philadelphia, once described as a city that rolls up its sidewalks at night, is earning a reputation instead for rolling out the red carpet to visitors as The Place That Loves You Back. Downtown tourist attractions, coupled with the cultural and historic treasures for which the city long has been known, have made Philadelphia a tremendously exciting and fun place to be. Philadelphia's remarkable recovery was dubbed by the New York Times as "one of the most stunning turnarounds in recent urban history."

Elected General Chair of the DNC on September 25, 1999, Mayor Rendell stresses the impact that the Democratic Party and its members make in the everyday lives of Philadephians, Pennsylvanians, and Americans.

Mayor Rendell and his wife, the Hon. Marjorie O. Rendell, an appellate judge of the Third Circuit U.S. Court of Appeals, live in the East Falls section of Philadelphia. Their son, Jesse, 19, is a sophomore at the University of Pennsylvania.

CHAPTER TWELVE

★

ELI SEGAL

★

HIS BOOK GREW OUT OF A CHALLENGE: to design and later implement national service legislation on a large scale. This experience stimulated our thinking about a role for business in social sector programs and taught us some of the pitfalls and possibilities of cross-sector partnerships. Our respective backgrounds — Eli's as a successful businessman with interests in publishing and direct mail, and Shirley's as the crafter of social programs for children and families — gave us insights into both private enterprise and the social sector. Our experience inspired us to explore this topic more deeply and to find a way to help others develop fruitful cross-sector partnerships.

Our paths first crossed in the White House early in 1993. Eli was a long-term friend of President Clinton, serving in the 1992 campaign as chief of staff. Shortly before the inaugural, he had been given responsibility for making good a campaign promise to give young Americans the chance to earn money for college by performing a year of service. He invited Shirley, the First Lady's policy advisor, to a meeting to plot strategy for the bill because she had drafted and helped to pass legislation creating a national service pilot program several years before.

The legislation that we and our colleagues put together challenged much of the conventional wisdom applied to federal social policy. Many federal programs provide specific dollars to specific types of nonprofit — generally state or local government — agencies to deliver specific services to a specific population in a specific way. The new national service program would specify the tool that would be provided — a person who would serve the community full-time for a year. But it would not specify the agency, the population to be served or the specific service to be provided, all of which would be defined locally.

Although many people, including the President, referred to the new national service program as the "domestic Peace Corps," it differed in an important respect. In the 1960s, when the Peace Corps was created, there was a presumption that the federal government ought to have a major role in solving local problems. The Peace Corps is today, as it was when it was enacted in 1961, a federally run program. Federal employees select, train, and assign Peace Corps volunteers to postings overseas, then supervise them during their term of service.

The legislation we worked on would establish a domestic Peace Corps in spirit, but not in design. A service program for the 1990s might spend federal dollars, but it would do so with state and local organizations at the helm. The nonprofit organizations managing the program would recruit and select team members, organize them and choose their service projects. They would receive a federal grant to pay team members a poverty-level stipend and team members would receive a federally funded award they could use to pay college expenses or student loans. But the federal government would not pay the full tab. To ensure that there was local support for the program, any organization that fielded teams would have to raise, in cash or through donations of goods and services, a portion of the funds it needed to operate the program.

In government jargon, these donations constitute "matching funds." Shirley's experience as a policymaker, working first as counsel for the Senate Labor and Human Resources Committee and later at the National Women's Law Center (a nonprofit women's legal policy organization) taught her that matching funds were a common feature of federal social programs. Federal policymakers like to make government dollars go further by requiring an organization to match a grant with additional sources of support.

But matching funds were often hard to come by, particularly in the mid-1990s, a time when state and local government dollars, like federal funds, were on the decline and the number of nonprofit organizations seeking support was on the rise. As a board member of several social sector organizations, Shirley knew leaders of many nonprofit organizations who spent at least a quarter of their time fundraising — cultivating contacts, drafting proposals, organizing events for donors. The idea of financially sustainable organizations that could solve seemingly intractable problems had great appeal. But where would these dollars come from?

Eli's experience in business gave him a different perspective. Eli had owned and run a series of profitable small- and medium-sized public and private companies since the middle of the 1970s. While he had served on the boards of a series of nonprofits, his business and pro bono lives were completely independent of each other until 1986, when a company he owned elected to sponsor a National Jigsaw Puzzle Championship. Conceived by the Dairy Barn, an entrepreneurial nonprofit in Athens, Ohio, as a way to fund its arts and crafts mission, the championship was born at the same time Eli was launching Bits & Pieces, a mail-order catalog featuring jigsaw puzzles. For Eli, sponsorship gave his fledgling catalog a cost-effective opportunity to achieve three objectives: develop a mailing list, create a "buzz" among puzzle aficionados and begin to build a visible national brand through television and newspaper coverage.

The partnership between Bits & Pieces and Dairy Barn was a success, strong enough for the parties to renew the relationship for a second year. Although Eli didn't dwell on it at the time, he was aware of the benefits of working with a nonprofit; the sponsorship gave his company the credibility and visibility he sought.

Reflecting on his experience, Eli believed it might be possible to attract private sector companies to support national service programs. A young program called City Year offered some evidence. City Year, based in Eli's hometown of Boston and founded by two of Shirley's law school classmates, had been created as an "action tank," designed to demonstrate that national service run by private organizations could be effective at teaching diverse teams of young people citizenship while meeting community needs. City Year's founders advocated a 50-50 public-private partnership, arguing that federal dollars should act as a "challenge grant," with every privately raised dollar matched by a federal one. We liked the idea. But when we briefed the president, he raised the concern that small grassroots organizations in low-income neighborhoods might have a hard time raising private funds. He asked us to establish a more modest matching requirement and then to find ways to encourage greater private sector support.

AmeriCorps, the new national service program, was born Sept. 23, 1993, just five months after the national service bill was introduced. That day would mark the beginning of a relentless effort to engage the business community in support for AmeriCorps. Consistent with the President's request, we had sought for the Corporation for National Service, the new federal corporation that would distribute the funding, the authority to solicit private funding. This capacity was unusual for agencies of the federal government, which could receive but not ask for donations unless specifically authorized to do so by legislation.

Eli was appointed to serve as the chief executive officer of the corporation for National Service and Shirley to serve as the managing director. We assembled a small team to help us reach out to business and foundations that could support local AmeriCorps programs.

Our major goal was to interest private-sector funders in supporting local AmeriCorps programs. We were open to receiving assistance in all forms, including corporate volunteers, professional expertise, donated equipment and supplies and job opportunities for AmeriCorps graduates. Our pitch was straightforward: AmeriCorps would tap the idealism and energy of a diverse group of Americans to benefit communities in tangible ways. They would tutor troubled students, restore natural habitats, organize neighborhood watch programs and help the homeless. AmeriCorps members themselves would have the chance to obtain a GED if they didn't have a high school diploma; earn money for college or graduate school; learn job skills; and develop problem solving, teamwork and leadership skills. By connecting local groups and mobilizing other volunteers in pursuit of common goals, AmeriCorps would build community. And finally, investors in this program would know at the end of the year what their money bought — how many hours of service were provided, how many people helped and what results could be attributed to AmeriCorps.

Our hope was that the AmeriCorps logo, because of the program's built-in competition among sponsors and high program selection criteria, would become a "Good Housekeeping Seal of Approval" of sorts.

Because this program was known to be a top priority of the President, it was not difficult to gain the attention of corporate leaders. But convincing them to invest turned out to be more time consuming and frustrating than Eli first imagined. Although we had structured the Corporation for National Service to operate more like a private corporation than a traditional bureaucracy, it was still a federal agency and funders were reluctant to donate directly to the government, even though their gifts were tax deductible. We had made it a policy not to pitch specific, local AmeriCorps programs to potential donors because as doing so would have been unfair to the other programs. But funders wanted help channeling their donations to AmeriCorps sponsors in their own communities or to those targeting specific issues. We wanted to explore whether we could license the AmeriCorps logo to companies for a fee. But the legal complexity inherent in doing so made this kind of arrangement impossible. Staff had many ideas about ways to engage the private sector and deluged us and the private sector outreach staff with requests for in-kind resources. But we found that it was just as time consuming to convince one company to donate 100 T-shirts as it was to raise $100,000 from another and our resources were spread thin.

Despite these challenges, the Corporation for National Service was able to persuade major businesses and foundations to support AmeriCorps. The General Electric Fund allocated $250,000 a year for AmeriCorps grantees, to be selected by local GE and United Way leaders in communities where GE had a substantial presence. American Airlines donated tickets to fly AmeriCorps members to training and helped with recruitment by airing public service announcements on its flights. Nike, through its PLAY initiative (Participate in the Lives of America's Youth) supported AmeriCorps members in six cities.

JP Morgan agreed to fund AmeriCorps Leaders, a cadre of national service graduates who would serve as team leaders in new AmeriCorps programs. Others in the AmeriCorps network were even more successful at generating support for the program. Washington State convinced Microsoft to wire all of the AmeriCorps programs in the state. City Year, already a leader in raising corporate support, was able to increase its size exponentially, from 100 young people serving each year to 1,000, by convincing private sector donors that their funds would be matched dollar for dollar. Between 1991 and 1998, City Year raised a total of $101 million, including $53.5 million from the private sector.

Serve Houston, a new program modeled on City Year, convinced local companies — Enron, Tenneco Gas, Shell Oil and others — to join in their annual Hands on Houston Day of Service. And in New Hampshire, three companies — Bank of New Hampshire, Providian Financial and Fleet Financial underwrote the cash matching requirements for all AmeriCorps programs in the state, while Health Source, a leading national HMO, provided health insurance and first aid training to New Hampshire AmeriCorps members.

Some national businesses and foundations became very involved. IBM, in partnership with Public Education Network, created Project First, which deployed AmeriCorps members and retired IBM executives to help public schools with their technology needs. The Ford Foundation made a grant of $3 million to the newly created Partnership for National Service and challenged this nonprofit to use the donation to leverage local funds, which it did at a rate of more that two to one. Sony Corporation ran public service announcements on its Times Square Jumbotron, organized a major concert in New York, and supported public safety programs in New York and Los Angeles. Larry Fish, chairman, president and CEO of Citizens Financial Network, a New England-based bank holding company, became chairman of the Rhode Island Commission on National Service and soon persuaded each university headquartered in Rhode Island to match each AmeriCorps education award to an incoming student with one of its own.

In the first year of AmeriCorps, the private sector contributed more than $40 million dollars. Although we regarded this as a success, we thought we would do more. We decided to require, not just encourage, local AmeriCorps sponsors to raise part of their matching funds from the private sector. Although no minimum amount was specified, local sponsors reacted with concern. Historically, some nonprofit organizations had existed solely with government funds, never receiving a single dollar from the private sector. Some AmeriCorps sponsors struggled with setting private sector fundraising policies, focusing on the negative — the types of business from which they would refuse to accept donations. Although we hoped to convince these reluctant AmeriCorps grantees that they could indeed tap this new source of revenue, we were reminded that sometimes the social sector and business sector were worlds apart. Nonetheless, with strong encouragement from the Corporation for National Service, AmeriCorps grantees did attract significant business and other private sector support and, as a group, were ultimately able to decrease the share of funds they derived from federal sources.

Eli left the Corporation in 1996 to test the idea of business-social sector partnerships with a new focus: welfare-to-work. In August 1996, welfare reform legislation was enacted. To help implement the new law, President Clinton called upon the business community to move welfare recipients into the workforce. Six months later, Eli formed the Welfare to Work Partnership with the CEOs of United Airlines, UPS, Burger King, Sprint and Monsanto. Their mission was simple: to help companies hire and retain welfare recipients without displacing other employees. When the Partnership was formally launched a few months later, the operating philosophy was in place: businesses could achieve their mission better with the help of the social sector. Most businesses had neither the experience nor the resources to do what primarily nonprofit workforce training and readiness organizations had done in decades. The partnership set out to help its members learn from the experience of others.

By the end of 1998, the Partnership consisted of more than 10,000 companies, large and small, across the country. It was working closely with national nonprofits and trade associations and trade associations like Goodwill Industries, the Council on Growing Companies, the National Retail Federation, the National Association of Manufacturers, the Enterprise Foundation, the U.S. Chamber of Commerce, the Society of Human Resource Managers and thousands of local nonprofit intermediaries.

Shirley left the Corporation for National Service in 1997 to become the founding executive director of a collaboration of a different sort. The nonprofit Learning First Alliance was formed by 12 national education agencies concerned with improving student learning in public schools. Together, the member organization represented more than 10 million individuals engaged in improving, providing and governing public education, including teachers, parents, school board members, administrators, state policymakers and teacher educators.

Experience suggested that the challenges faced by Alliance members as they tried to work together to achieve their goals were not unique: agreeing on goals and priorities, ensuring equal ownership and establishing decision making mechanisms. Nor were they insurmountable, even though the collaboration included labor and management, regulators and practitioners, parents and administrators.

One topic the group wrestled with almost more than any other was working with corporate sponsors. The organizations had widely varying policies themselves — one refused corporate dollars altogether; another received more than $1 million a year from corporate sponsorships. Several had strong concerns about taking money from businesses that had positions on legislation that conflicted with their own, and others were concerned about appearing to endorse a company's products. Again, although the group was ultimately able to raise corporate funding, the issues it faced underscore the many challenges that nonprofits confront in developing business partnerships.

As Shirley discussed her experience at the Learning First Alliance with Eli, we found that we had developed similar ideas about what makes partnerships successful. Our experiences with both business and social sector organizations — we collectively have served on the board or staff of 21 nonprofit organizations, 15 businesses and four government organizations — convinced us there is a need to demystify cross-sector partnerships. The majority of individuals in the business sector have little to do with their counterparts in the social sector and vice versa. Business and social sector leaders travel in different worlds and usually deep suspicion exists. Even individuals with extensive experience developing partnerships and collaboration within their own fields have difficulty applying those lessons across the sectors.

In the course of our travels, we have met visionary individuals whose good instincts, creative energy, and ability to think strategically have made them innovators in the world of cross-sector partnerships. Mission-driven, they have worked to bridge the divide, learning about the other sector and reaching out to potential partners.

The individuals seemed, as we spoke with them, to have followed similar paths to developing partnerships, even though they varied in the kind of business or social sector group they represented. Their stories, we felt, might be useful to others interested in exploring cross-sector partnerships.

In studying these issues further, we also discovered an extensive body of literature describing the creation of alliances within the business sector and the building of collaborations within the social sector. As we reviewed the literature from both fields, we found common themes and lessons communicated in very different languages that accorded with our own research and experience. But although some of the material we looked at included references to working across the sectors, this was not its primary purpose.

This book introduces businesspeople and nonprofit managers to cutting-edge cross sector partnerships. It teaches the lessons we have gleaned from our own experience, written materials and more than 100 interviews with individuals on both sides of cross-sector partnerships. We chose to focus on the social sector, which we define as including both nonprofit and government organizations with a mission of meeting human needs. Nonetheless most of our analysis would apply just as well to other types of government or nonprofit institutions — such as those working in the arts or on environmental issues. We have tried to use the term nonprofit when the analysis applies specifically to not-for-profit, nongovernmental organizations.

ELI SEGAL

Eli Segal currently serves as President and CEO of the Welfare to Work Partnership. Located in Washington, D.C., the Partnership is a national, nonpartisan effort on the part of the business community to help move people on public assistance into private-sector jobs.

Mr. Segal served as Assistant to President Bill Clinton from January 1993 to February 1996. In this capacity, he was responsible for the design and enactment of the legislation that created AmeriCorps. In October 1993, Mr. Segal was confirmed by the U.S. Senate to the additional position of CEO of the Corporation for National Service, a post he held until October 1995.

Mr. Segal is a successful small business entrepreneur who applies his knowledge of the for-profit sector to his work with social sector organizations. Prior to 1992, he served as President of several consumer product companies, including the American Publishing Corporation and Bits & Pieces, Inc. Most recently, he was the Publisher of "Games" magazine.

Mr. Segal sits in several nonprofit and corporate boards of directors, including the Board of Overseers of the Heller School of Brandeis University. He is also Chair of the University of Michigan Center for Learning Through Community Service and Co-chair of the National Alliance to End Homelessness.

CHAPTER THIRTEEN

★

JONATHAN TISCH

THE POWER OF PARTNERSHIPS

When the Democratic Party was founded more than 200 years ago, it was with the notion that individuals needed to come together and work collectively on issues and challenges that were too big to be confronted alone.

Encompassing a range of subjects, such as safety and security, the economy, or environmental issues, the Democratic Party has long positioned itself on the side of everyday people — trying to enhance their quality of life.

And, while times and conditions have changed over the years, that lofty but worthwhile goal has remained a constant, guiding principle of the Party. A sense of responsibility to our fellow citizens and to our communities is one of the most important aspects of our Party's platform and agenda. It is the principle that attracted me to the Democratic Party and one that I hope we can inspire all Americans to support.

While some people speak about the relationship between government and community in terms of "giving back," I prefer to think of it as something much more significant. For me, it transcends the attitude of a one time "you do for me, and I'll do for you." It goes beyond writing a check, putting on a tuxedo and going to a charity dinner.

It is about understanding one's responsibility.

That notion is one that John Gardiner, former Secretary of Health, Education and Welfare and founder of Common Cause, means when he describes The Democratic Compact, "Freedom and responsibility, liberty and duty. That's the deal."

As we look to fulfill that notion, we can refer to the three tenets of creating a civil society: Opportunity; Responsibility; Community

Of course, as a part of that discussion, each one of us must ask ourselves:

• What do I owe myself?

• What do I owe those around me?

• What do I owe society?

To begin answering those questions, I'd like to refer to a notion that I often speak about and a philosophy that is at the core of how we at Loews Hotels operate — The Power of Partnerships.

In its basic form, the concept is about putting aside individual differences and concerns and working towards a common goal.

Well, I can't think of a more important partnership than the one between government and the people it serves.

Today, while the country is experiencing unprecedented prosperity, due in large part, in my opinion, to the leadership of President Clinton, Vice-President Gore and former Treasury Secretary Robert Rubin, we still have many challenges.

And while our nation is projected to have a surplus of $1.47 trillion over the next 10 years, the economic and political realities are such that we cannot and should not expect government to solve all our problems — Certainly not on its own.

To that end, I believe the key to our mutual success lies in our ability to expand the partnership between the public and private sectors in several key areas.

⁓

Economic Development

In my business, the travel and tourism industry, public/private partnerships have played a vital role as a catalyst for new hotel development. In most cases, the projects would likely not have come to fruition without government incentives and involvement.

More specifically, at Loews Hotels, two of our newest properties — Loews Miami Beach Hotel and Loews Philadelphia Hotel — were developed in partnership with their respective cities.

It is important to note that this is not corporate welfare — the incentives that were offered were needed to attract economic development. The end result for the cities has been job creation and tax revenues.

In Miami Beach, the lack of upscale hotel space to accommodate the beautiful Miami Beach Convention Center meant that the convention center was underutilized and that the city was losing lucrative business. As a result, the city initiated a comprehensive search to find a partner for the City of Miami Beach, which owns the convention center, to build a new 800-room luxury convention hotel.

When the process first began in the mid-'90s, the market was still very soft and the city couldn't find a partner that was willing to take the risk alone. So the City Commission worked to develop an incentive package that had every major hotel company responding to the request for proposals, touching off a highly competitive bid.

Well, in the end, Loews Hotels was chosen and I am pleased to note that the new property, Loews Miami Beach Hotel, has indeed served as a catalyst to draw some important conventions and trade shows to the city, pumping millions of dollars into the economy. Specifically, the City of Miami Beach has projected that it will generate more than $1 billion of economic activity for the area in its first 10 years of operation.

This is also due in large part to the multiplier effect that travel and tourism has on the economy. When people are traveling, they are also eating in restaurants, using transportation, sightseeing and visiting cultural area attractions.

In Philadelphia, former Mayor Ed Rendell, was such a firm believer in the significant impact travel and tourism can have on the city's economic well-being and survival that he made a commitment to build 2,000 new hotel rooms by the year 2000.

Along with generating more than 3,200 full-time jobs, the new hotel supply is also expected to have a tremendous impact on the city's economy on a more long-term basis as it draws larger conventions and trade shows to the newly-expanded Pennsylvania Convention Center.

The Loews Philadelphia Hotel, which opened in April 2000, also has a lot of historic significance. It represents the conversion of a national historic landmark, the PSFS Building, originally opened in 1932 and considered to be one of the most important skyscrapers in the country, into a luxury 583-room convention headquarters hotel.

Given that the building had been vacant for quite some time, and was not able to be used for either office space or for residential use, the concept of transforming it into a hotel was an ideal solution. Our project not only brought back to life an important and treasured building, it helped change the dynamic and feel of a neighborhood that had been largely ignored.

Helping to ensure that our hotel, as well as several others in the area, came to fruition was the goal of the Philadelphia Industrial Development Corporation (PIDC) which provided a $3.25 million loan for our project and also helped finance nine other hotels in the city. Specifically for Loews Philadelphia Hotel, this also included $20.75 million of HUD 108 loans.

Miami Beach and Philadelphia are two examples of how a public/private partnership can create economic development, jobs and tax revenue. If the public and private sectors did not work together, these projects would not have proceeded. Furthermore, these projects served as catalysts for subsequent developments in these cities.

Community Involvement

In addition to the long-term economic benefits that public/private partnerships can create, we at Loews Hotels also believe in making a positive difference in the communities where we operate our hotels.

Hotels are a somewhat unique business in that we are open 24 hours a day, seven days a week, 365 days a year. We cannot pick up and move the property if it is not performing well. To that end, I believe it is incumbent on us — and on all corporate citizens — to be responsive to the needs and challenges of the communities where we operate.

Specifically at Loews Hotels, we try to fulfill those responsibilities through the Good Neighbor Policy. When the program was formally launched in 1991, it set a precedent as the first and most comprehensive community outreach program of its kind in the hospitality industry. Stemming from our longstanding tradition of being responsive to the needs of the communities where our properties are located, the program was introduced to further extend the company's efforts to address various issues of social concern.

Using the resources that are intrinsic to a hotel's daily operation, the program's goal is to utilize hotels in a manner that can also have a positive impact on their communities. Specific activities that each hotel is required to fulfill include donating excess food to local food banks, shelters and hunger relief programs, supporting local literacy programs by providing space for the classes to be held and volunteer instructors from the hotels, donating used goods, such as linens and furniture to local organizations and shelters as well as extensive recycling programs.

While the most gratifying aspect of the program is the positive difference it has made on the lives of so many people across the country, we are also proud that the Good Neighbor Policy was honored on 1996 with the President's Service Award from the Points of Light Foundation, the highest honor the President can give for corporate responsibility.

In keeping with that commitment, Loews Hotels has also taken a lead role in one of the country's most timely important social issues — Welfare to Work.

When President Clinton signed the Welfare Reform Act in 1996, he said that we were "ending welfare as we know it." In order for this country to move more than 4 million people from welfare to work, the business community had to take the lead.

~~

Welfare to Work

That reality led to the formation of The Welfare to Work Partnership — of which I am proud to serve as Vice Chair. Formed three years ago by five companies — UPS, Burger King, United Airlines, Monsanto and Sprint — today there are more than 20,000 businesses that are members. Considering that there are hundreds of thousands of able-bodied, enthusiastic, work-ready welfare recipients looking to re-enter the mainstream economy at a time unemployment is at record low levels, welfare to work juxtaposes the sometimes opposing goals of doing what is right for business with what is right for society.

As the country experiences the lowest unemployment rate in three decades — 4.1 percent for the nation — almost every business is feeling the affects and facing the challenge of finding people to fill jobs.

The travel and tourism industry, which is the country's second largest employer, is certainly feeling the impact. But we are not alone. This is an issue that is affecting all areas of the economy, from the service sector to manufacturing, agriculture, high tech and health care, companies large and small are experiencing the same dilemma — where to find employees.

The subject is so significant that in recent testimony before Congress, Federal Reserve Chairman Alan Greenspan called the worker shortage issue "the greatest single threat to the continued American economic vitality."

The shrinking pool of available workers cannot satisfy the world's demand for American goods and services. And, as the competition for those people grows, we need to do more than put up a help wanted sign.

At Loews Hotels we are doing just that. Approximately 10 percent of our employees at our newest hotel, the Loews Philadelphia Hotel, are former welfare recipients. And in South Florida, Loews Miami Beach Hotel helped form a consortium, with 44 other hotels of the Greater Miami & The Beaches

Hotel Association, to transition up to 300 former welfare recipients into the lodging industry within three years.

On a national basis, the Welfare to Work Partnership has achieved great success in its efforts to provide companies with information and resources on how to transition former welfare recipients into their business.

For example:

- Nearly 1.1 Million former welfare recipients now have jobs as a result of the legislation signed by President Clinton in 1997.
- 62 percent of companies that have hired former welfare recipients indicate that retention rates are equal to or better than non-welfare employees.
- 80 percent of companies find them to be "good, productive employees."

Having had the pleasure of getting to know some of the former welfare recipients now working at Loews Hotels, I can confirm that last statistic from first hand experience. The Welfare to Work program has truly enabled us to tap into a wonderful group of employees who simply needed some support to get them back into the workforce.

Welfare reform is another example of how the public and private sector can work together to affect positive change in people's live. Government action created the need to move people from welfare to work within a number of years. The private sector accepted responsibility and stepped up and hired hundreds of thousands of good, productive employees. The government continued to understand its role and offered incentives for businesses with Work Opportunity and Welfare to Work tax credits.

The public and private sector must continue to work together on important issues related to welfare to work, including child-care and transportation, so that progress can continue. Neither sector will be able to solve these remaining problems alone.

Worker Shortage

In keeping with the subject of attracting and keeping great employees, I also understand the need and, more importantly, the benefits of viewing a company's relationship with its employees as a partnership.

In the very competitive hospitality industry, the only real way to differentiate ourselves from the competition is through service. And, because the day-to-day contact with our guests isn't made by me or any of the other senior executives, but by the people who are out there on the front lines, we must view them as partners and treat them with the respect that relationship requires.

To help foster that relationship, we believe it is important to invest in our employees. Loews Hotels has created a comprehensive training program that is aimed at establishing an atmosphere in which our employees are empowered to act in the best interest of our guests, customers and, because we are after all a business — the bottomline. Taking that notion one step further, we recently introduced Loews University — a program available to all of our employees to help them continue to learn, grow and advance — not only professionally, but personally.

As a way to recognize the achievements of our front-line employees, we acknowledge the employee of the year from each property with our Loews Legends program. Each "legend" is invited with a guest for a weekend in New York City that included a special dinner and tribute, as well as financial awards to recognize their contributions. We also take out a full-page as in USA Today recognizing these individuals for all their worthy endeavors.

Bringing this chapter full circle, I hope you can see the benefits — the power — of partnerships, whether they are with government, communities or employees.

As we look towards the future and work for continued economic prosperity for all, we must remember the founding principle of the Democratic Party. By working in partnership — we can continue to be on the side of the individual — and together, we can help make our lives and communities better.

———

JONATHAN TISCH

Jonathan M. Tisch was named President of Loews hotels in 1986 and assumed the role of Chief Executive Officer in 1989. In addition, as part of a management succession plan that was announced in November 1998, Tisch was appointed to the newly created Office of the President for the Hotel's parent company — Loews Corporation. Tisch also serves on the Corporation's Board of Directors.

During his tenure, Tisch has been instrumental in overseeing the company's growth and subsequent emergence as one of the leading luxury hotel chains. Blending a cutting edge approach to marketing and operations with a conservative development philosophy, he is recognized as one of the industry's leading authorities.

Underscoring his presence as an industry leader, Tisch served a five-year term as an officer of the American Hotel & Motel Association, culminating in his Chairmanship of the organization in 1997. Since 1995, Tisch has also served as Chairman of the travel business Roundtable — a prominent coalition of chief executives representing various sectors of the travel and tourism industry. Also since 1995, he has served as the Chairman of the Annual NYU International Hospitality Industry Investment Conference, considered to be one of the premier forums for the lodging industry's highest ranking executives.

Taking a lead role in one of the nation's current social issues, Tisch was named Vice Chair of The Welfare to Work partnership — a group of businesses helping transition people from welfare to work — in February 2000. He had previously served on the Board of Directors. He also serves on the President's Export council, which provides a forum for addressing trade issues affecting U.S. businesses.

Actively involved in several community and philanthropic activities, he currently serves on the board of Trustees for Tufts University, as well as the Board of Directors of the Elizabeth Glaser Pediatric AIDS Foundation, the VH1 Save the Music Foundation and the National Academy of Recording Arts & Sciences Foundation (NARAS). Tisch also serves on the Advisory Board of the Urban Policy Center at Columbia University and the Business Council for the Metropolitan Museum of Art. In addition, he is on the Board and is the Treasurer of the New York Giants.

As a result of Tisch's leadership and dedication to the travel industry, as well as for his commitment to social responsibility and community outreach, he has received numerous honors and accolades. Among them, he has been named one of the Business Travel Industry's Most Influential Executives by "Business Travel News" for five consecutive years, one of

"Crain's New York Business" magazine's All Stars, and most recently, Tisch was named as one of "Hospitality Design's" Industry 20, a selection of individuals who represent lodging's most innovative and cutting edge leaders. In addition, he was named as one of the 25 Most Influential People in the Meetings Industry, by "Meeting News" magazine.

An outspoken opponent of regressive legislative issues affecting the travel industry, Tisch is credited as one of the major forces behind the successful effort to repeal New York's onerous hotel occupancy tax, setting a precedent for other cities that considered targeting hotels for additional levies.

Continually seeking opportunities to boost New York City's image as the mecca for the entertainment industry, he spearheaded several efforts to bring the Grammy Awards to the City and has served as Chairman of the New York Host Committee in 1994, 1992, and 1988. In recognition of his commitment to New York City, Tisch was named recipient of the 1995 New Yorker for New York award given by The Citizens Committee for New York City. He also received the 1995 New York Society of Association Executives' Outstanding New Yorker award for his many contributions to New York.

Tisch also received a Special Achievement Award from the Larry King Cardiac Foundation in 1997 for his numerous civic and philanthropic endeavors. And, in 1995, he was named as one of the 1995 honorees of The Ability First Awards, given by Just One Break, a non-profit employment organization for people with disabilities.

Recognized for his leadership, Tisch has been a keynote or guest speaker at the Wharton School of Business at the University of Pennsylvania, Central Florida University, Johnson & Wales University, Cornell University, as well as for numerous business and community organizations. In his remarks, Tisch elaborates on the "Power of Partnerships" and the importance of establishing dedicated and deep rooted business relationships with employees, customers, and the community at large.

A graduate of Tufts University with a Degree in Political Science, Tisch was the recipient of the Alumni Association's 1996 Distinguished Alumni Award. During his years in Boston, Tisch's affection for the television and film industry was ignited. He received two Emmy nominations for his work as a Cinematographer/Producer at WBZ-TV. And as a member of the Screen Actors Guild, Tisch has made several cameo appearances in television shows and feature films

Loews Hotels currently owns and/or operates 15 hotels and resorts in the U.S. and Canada. As part of the largest expansion in the chain's history, the company has recently opened three new properties and has three more in various stages of development. These include the first ever House of Blues Hotel, a Loews Hotel, a 367-room property located in Chicago's Marina City that opened in October 1998 and the Loews Miami Beach Hotel, an 800-room property that opened in December 1998. And as part of a joint venture with Universal, Inc. and the Rank Organization, Loews Hotels opened the first of three hotels located at Universal Studios Escape in Orlando. The 750-room Portofino bay Hotel at Universal Orlando, a Loews Hotel, opened in September 1999. That will be followed by the 650-room Hard Rock Hotel at Universal Orlando in January 2001, and the 1,000 room Royal Pacific Resort at Universal Orlando, a Loews Hotel, in 2001. The most recent opening was the April 2000 debut of the 583-room Loews Philadelphia Hotel, which was the conversion of the landmark PSFS building. Under development is a new 400-room Loews Boston Hotel in the theater district that is scheduled to open in 2002.

CHAPTER FOURTEEN

★

ANDREW
TOBIAS

NET WORTH IS NICE,
BUT SELF WORTH IS EVEN NICER

*i*magine my surprise — I am treasurer of the Democratic National Committee — when I got in this week's mail a certificate from my counterpart, the treasurer of the Republican National Committee, in recognition of my "proven commitment and dedication to the Republican Party." It came along with a four-page fundraising letter and was suitable for framing.

Direct mail inanities can befall anyone, and perhaps I should take this opportunity to apologize for anything inane you may have gotten from us. I mention my RNC certificate simply as proof that I am not one of those people who would never, ever vote for a Republican. Having once or twice in the past sent checks to Republicans (I was young! I was foolish!) I have ever since gotten warm personal letters from the most remarkable people. Newt Gingrich was writing me for a while. The chairman of Christian Voice has written me more than once to warn me — in the most strident terms — against . . . well, people like me.

Anyway, my point is that I don't consider myself a mindless partisan, even though I grew up in a Democratic household (Dad would occasionally vote Republican, to our mild horror, but Mom would cancel him out). And I don't agree with everything Democrats have ever done, although I think our intentions were usually good. Nor am I in lockstep with some of our strongest allies — mainly our friends in the Trial Bar. In my view, they have done a lot of good (have you seen "Erin Brockovich?" read A *Civil Action?*), but in at least one area — auto insurance reform — we have a deep, deep disagreement.

Why am I telling you all this?

Because I believe this is the most important election of our lives, and that those of us who might not ordinarily consider themselves terribly political, let alone partisan, should do everything we can to assure a resounding Democratic victory in November. And that includes my Republican friends. Because what I think has happened is that the whole landscape has shifted to the right. Our party certainly still has its extreme liberals — and God bless 'em. But by and large, we have moved to the center.

The leadership of the other party, by contrast, has moved so far right it's almost fallen over the edge. A moderate Republican couldn't even get confirmed as ambassador to Mexico, let alone be considered as a viable presidential candidate.

Yes, I have a fair number of Republican friends. But they're not *Trent Lott* Republicans. They're not Tom Delay or Jesse Helms or *Bob Barr* Republicans. So my pitch to my Republican friends — some of whom have even given me nice big checks for the Democratic Party — is, "help us help you get your party back."

The irony is that on the one bedrock Republican issue — fiscal prudence — the Republican leadership has totally lost its mind. At a time when the economy has never been stronger — exactly the time you *don't* want to add fuel to the fire — George W. Bush pushes over and over for a massive tax cut that sensible people like Alan Greenspan (a Republican) think would be terrible economic policy, and that even conservative Republicans like John McCain have attacked for being far too heavily weighted in favor of the rich.

I happen to be one of those rich. But I don't think it's fair. And I don't want to live in a country where, ultimately, the top 5 percent will be guarded from everyone else by sentries with machine guns. I was flown to a country like that to give a speech once. Inside the Hyatt we were feasting on lobster and champagne. Soldiers manned the entrance to protect us.

Obviously, the other party doesn't aim for that kind of country either. Not even Trent Lott. (Plus, they may figure that in America we can *all* have machine guns — thank heavens for the gun show loophole they don't want to close — so we won't need the soldiers.) But really: is this a time for massive tax cuts for Steve Forbes? Wouldn't it be more prudent, and ultimately better for our kids and their kids, if we used much of our surplus to pay down a good chunk of the multi-trillion debt we accumulated in the Reagan/Bush years? I've long argued we don't have to pay it *all* off — a healthy country need not be debt-*free*. But this is a perfect time, when times are good, to pay it down. And if we can afford a moderate tax cut, aimed mostly at middle America not the rich, all the better.

Amazingly, we Democrats have become the party of fiscal responsibility. Not every last Congressman and Senator is on the same page. But most are. The Clinton/Gore administration made a very clear choice for fiscal prudence right from the start, and it has paid off big time.

Many of my Republican friends say, hold on! Are you giving Clinton/Gore credit for the economic good times?

And my answer is . . . yes. At least in good measure.

Sure, 95 percent of the credit goes to the American people, and to the terrific innovators and entrepreneurs and risk takers who've made the last several years so great. But that's always true. What's also true is that the government has the power to screw it up. And frequently has. And the Clinton/Gore administration *didn't*.

I urge my skeptical friends to read Bob Woodward's 1994 best-seller, *The Agenda*. No paean to the administration, this was a book sold on the morning talk shows as portraying the sophomoric chaos in the new White House. You know: guys in their twenties pulling all-nighters. But what the book is really about was the first budget. That was the plot line! The budget! It showed the struggle, both within the White House and to a certain extent within the President's own mind, between well-intentioned liberals who wanted, now that we had the White House, to tax and spend to save the world; and the equally well-intentioned but more practical idealists who believed that first you had to satisfy the bond market and get the economy going in the right direction.

In hindsight, it's easy to take the last seven years' prosperity for granted. But I believe that if the President — with the strong urging of the Vice-President, who was an early advocate of this practical idealism — had failed to make the right choice, my net worth would not be what it is today. Or, very possibly, yours. Nor the unemployment figure. Nor the budget surplus. Nor the reduced crime rate to which a good economy contributes.

And do you know how many Republican votes that first Clinton/Gore budget got in Congress?

Take a guess, because this is an important question.

Not one.

The budget carried only because, back then (it seems like ancient history), the Democrats held a majority in Congress.

Nor was that all. On top of its fiscal prudence, the Clinton/Gore administration, with the backing of a lot of Democrats in Congress, pushed aggressively for freer trade. It was a huge fight, and you may remember a little man with big ears talking incessantly, and dismissively, about the "giant sucking sound" NAFTA would produce if we were so foolish as to pass it. Our unemployment rate would soar.

But it was good policy, and it, along with our other trade policies, have served the American people well — along with people in other countries, whom we should also want to see prosper.

What Democrats get, I think, perhaps better than the other party's leadership — which typically takes such relish in bashing our tiny foreign aid budget, and which seemed so proud to have killed the Comprehensive Test-Ban Treaty — is this: That in an increasingly interdependent world, if "they" do better, we do better, too.

If "they" do better, we do better, too.

It is a message of inclusion, of fairness, of opportunity and community.

That's why I was so proud of the Democrats for pushing to hike the minimum wage from $4.25 to $5.15 in 1996. The other party initially said no, you can't do that. What we needed, said the other party, was a big tax cut for the wealthy, not a hike in the minimum wage. Raising the minimum wage, they said, would throw poor people out of work and drive employers out of business. And it was inflationary to boot. Even after the bill was sweetened with $20 billion in tax cuts to ease the alleged impact on business, 92 Republicans voted against it.

The Democrats, by contrast, thought these concerns were wildly overblown, and that simple fairness, in any event, required that we take the risk. Well, as you know, the minimum wage *was* hiked, and, in the years since, we have experienced the *lowest* unemployment and the *lowest* inflation in decades.

Obviously, you can't raise the minimum wage to $30 an hour — that wouldn't work. You can, though, I think, raise it to $6.50, as the Democrats now propose — a whopping $13,000 a year. Doing so helps people who typically have very little bargaining power of their own. And, at the margin, it helps make work more attractive than welfare, idleness or crime. Even Henry Ford — no communist — believed he should pay his workers enough so they could afford to buy his cars.

If "they" do better, we do better, too.

So does it make sense to abandon the successful Clinton/Gore course we've been on?

No one can guarantee continued prosperity; but I liken it to any other very successful large enterprise. If the CEO is retiring and has been working in tight partnership for 7 years with a very effective, behind-the-scenes, COO ... and if the CEO strongly recommends that COO as his successor ... why on earth would the board of directors (that's us) look outside the company to a guy whose experience and aptitude seem less impressive. This is, along with everything else, after all, as the President is fond of saying, *a job*. It is in fact, and by far, the most important executive position in the world.

I would like to see Al Gore and Joe Lieberman in the White House because I would like to see continued economic progress. A few more years of this and even I, world's cheapest man, may stop buying used cars. (If you didn't know, I have long preached that "that new-car smell is the most expensive fragrance in the world.")

But forget all that. Assume, if you want, that George W. is just as experienced, capable, and solid as Al Gore. Assume there is no economic risk in switching gears. Your net worth will be just as robust either way. That's a lot to assume, if you ask me, but go ahead.

What good is net worth without self worth?

Appreciation of your stock portfolio without, also, a sense that you are appreciated as a person?

And this is where, to me, Bill Clinton and Al Gore have been true heroes.

They have said time and again, in words and actions, that "America doesn't have a person to waste."

They and the Democratic Party welcome and celebrate diversity. The leadership of the other party seems less enthusiastic.

Picture the contrast.

The President's cabinet and top advisors walk into the House Chamber to attend the State of the Union address and it looks like America. You've got your whites and your blacks and your Latinos, your men and your women, your Jews and your gentiles, your guy in a wheelchair.

The top six officers of the Democratic National Committee walk into a room and you've got your brilliant African-American mayor (previous to his election named most respected judge in his state), your dynamic Latina congresswoman, your coupla terrific WASPy guys, your coupla women, your coupla Jews, and your gay guy. (Adds to more than six due to overlap.)

The thirteen Republican House managers walk into the room for their impeachment proceeding and you've got . . . thirteen white guys.

This is not to knock white guys. My boyfriend's a white guy. (And, like all 13 of the Republican House managers, Christian.) Nor is it to say the President's cabinet or the DNC leadership is *completely* representative — nor for a moment to suggest any of this should be done based on some kind of formula or quota. It shouldn't!

It's just that most Democrats genuinely believe that many of our most talented citizens *are* different from the straight white Christian males who have traditionally held all the top jobs. Many Republicans believe this, too, but it does not seem to animate the Republican leadership.

Trent Lott, who runs the Senate, has likened gay Americans to kleptomaniacs. Dick Armey refers to his House colleague Barney Frank as "Barney fag." Governor Bush tells a group of religious leaders he would not knowingly hire openly gay Americans if he were elected, but that — being compassionate — he would not fire someone subsequently discovered to be gay solely for that reason. "We won't knowingly hire Jews, but if Secretary of State Madeleine Albright *turns out* to be Jewish, we won't fire her just for that." *Can you imagine anyone saying such a thing?* Obviously not. But that's different, says the Republican leadership. Why? Because, well, gays are second-class citizens who should hide who they are and, better still, simply choose to be straight like everyone else. (Being straight or gay is a choice, Bush running mate Dan Quayle forcefully assured us the last time around. And perhaps for him it was. But most people do not choose their sexual orientation.)

It was only 79 years ago that women in this country got the vote. By now, almost everyone thinks it's a good idea — even though the Bible says women should be subservient (and non-virgin brides, stoned to death in the public square). Until just 35 years ago, African Americans were still officially second-class citizens in parts of America. By now, happily, most of that is ancient history — even though the Bible says, "slaves, obey thy masters" (Colossians) "with fear and trembling" (Ephesians).

And until just 8 years ago, the issue of fairness and equality for gays and lesbians had never been placed on the national agenda. Today, much of mainstream America has come to know us as their friends and neighbors, sons and daughters, colleagues, employers and employees. The Republican leadership has yet to get this one right, though I believe eventually they will.

A couple of years ago I was with Joe Andrew, who is now national chair of the DNC, when he was asked to make a few impromptu remarks at a fancy dinner in Los Angeles. The city was strutting its stuff for us, hoping to be selected as the site for the 2000 Democratic Convention, and this big outdoor dinner was part of the show. Asked by the Mayor to say a few words, Joe — who I think had had a glass of wine — said something so completely unscripted and natural and from the heart, that I have been quoting it ever since. "You know," he said, "*we're Democrats*. We don't care whether you're black or you're white or you're green or you're purple. We don't care whether you walked in here or you *rolled* in here. We don't care what religion you are or what *gender* you are or what gender you hold hands with — so long as you hold hands."

And that's the deal. *So long as you hold hands*. We are one magnificently diverse country. Opportunity for all; special privilege for none; a community that encourages the best in all of us. The Democrats really mean it.

⎯⎯

PS - Ralph Nader. Listen, I have to say something about this, too. I used to idolize Ralph Nader. I marveled at his courage in taking on the auto industry on issues of safety. I was thrilled to see my dad, who ran an ad agency, do the first full-page ads, pro-bono, to launch Nader's Public Citizen and his Congress Project. I have those ads framed in my office. I was over the moon when Nader gave a blurb for my 1982 expose of the insurance industry. We consumers have a lot to thank Ralph Nader for.

And yet it turns out to my great dismay, there is another side to Ralph

Nader. I could write 10,000 words about this — and did not so long ago. In the one area I had come to know in painstaking detail — your overpriced, rotten automobile insurance — Consumers Union has been crying out for meaningful reform since 1962 ... and Ralph Nader, of all people, has been without question the lynchpin in preventing it.

We all want heroes. It was very discouraging for me to see how much harm Nader had — inadvertently, I'm sure — caused drivers and accident victims.

But that was nothing compared with what he is doing now. His candidacy could actually siphon off enough votes to throw the White House to the Republicans for the next four years and shape the Supreme Court for the next 25. *Nothing* could be worse for the little guy Nader claims to represent. And yet mutual friends assure me that he's in the race to stay, consequences be damned. ("The Democrats could use a four-year cold shower," he told Tim Russert on Meet the Press when asked about this. And if it's a 25-year cold shower because of the Court, and young women have to go back to coat-hanger abortions, well, that doesn't seem to bother Nader either.)

Ultimately, we will win. We have to. But if we don't, and women lose the right to choose and consumer protections are given lip service and global warming is ignored and tax breaks are directed toward the rich while earned-income credits are scaled back ... if the NRA rejoices and the tobacco industry exhales a sigh of relief ... Ralph Nader could turn out to have been one of the most destructive characters of all time.

PPS - I almost forgot. I'm treasurer of the DNC. *We take credit cards!* Before you turn the page, how about logging on to www.democrats.org and pitching in?

———◆———

ANDREW TOBIAS

Andrew Tobias majored in "Slavic languages and literatures" at Harvard but spent most of his time running the million-dollar student business conglomerate and publishing Let's Go: The Student Guide To Europe.

After graduating in 1968, he landed a vice president's spot at then-hot/then-not National Student Marketing Corporation, about which he wrote The Funny Money Game, his first book to gain national attention; then fled back to Harvard for his MBA.

He has written hundreds of magazine pieces for New York Magazine, Esquire, Time, Parade and Worth, among others, but is best known for his books — among them, The Only Investment Guide You'll Ever Need, which has sold more than a million copies, and The Best Little Boy in the World, which was added to the Modern Library series to mark the twenty-fifth anniversary of its original, pseudonymous publication.

His software, Managing Your Money, was one of the personal computer industry's early best-sellers. With Jane Bryant Quinn, he co-hosted Beyond Wall Street, an eight-part 1997 PBS documentary.

Tobias has won the Gerald Loeb Award for Excellence in Financial Journalism and the Consumer Federation of America Media Service Award. His anti-smoking commercials have run throughout the former Soviet Union. His work on auto insurance reform led to the placement of three initiatives on the March 1996 California ballot. His daily comment appears at www.andrewtobias.com. He currently serves as treasurer of the Democratic National Committee.

CHAPTER FIFTEEN

★

KATHLEEN
KENNEDY TOWNSEND

LEADERSHIP FOR AN AGE OF DISCOVERY

hanks to Bill Clinton and Al Gore, and the hard work and imagination of the American people, we've built the greatest era of prosperity and progress ever.

We've brought the federal budget into surplus and buried the label of 'tax and spend' By bringing crime down for eight consecutive years, we've gained the trust of the American people to fight crime. More Americans trust our party to combat violence than the Republicans. We have eliminated the shame of lifelong welfare dependency from millions of American's lives and begun to restore for them the dignity of work. Teen pregnancy is at an all-time low. Home ownership is at an all-time high.

All across our country, Democrats are revitalizing our communities with innovative, effective answers to our nation's most critical challenges. We are drawing citizens into the search for solutions, engaging their best efforts, and we are getting results. When we apply the Democratic problem-solving approach, we move our country forward on the issues that matter most to Americans. This is a revolution in how government, communities, and citizens face up to the challenges of our lives. Not just Election Day, but everyday.

In Maryland, for instance, we are fundamentally changing the way we attack crime and drugs. We're focusing on the neighborhoods hardest hit by crime, the HotSpots, and we're hitting back with a results-oriented strategy using teams of citizens, police, prosecutors, parole and probation agents, schools, religious leaders, and businesses. HotSpots have helped crime fall in Maryland at twice the national average.

Not only are we bringing crime down, we are reinvigorating a sense of mission and purpose among law enforcement and government bureaucrats. In our HotSpots, we brought parole and probation officers out of their offices and into the neighborhoods where the people they supervise live. I can't tell you how many have said to me that this has changed their life. This is why they went into probation work in the first place, and now they're on the street and seeing the difference they make on a neighborhood.

And we are restoring our citizens' faith, confidence, and connection to their government. A few months ago, a group from Johns Hopkins came to a school just a few blocks away to talk to the children about careers. For the first time in anyone's memory, children, and a lot of them, said they wanted to be police officers when they grew up. They no longer saw the police as "that guy who locked up my brother." They see them as honored members of the community who make a real difference. Those are young people who are going to steer clear from violence and drugs, and they're going to keep their friends on the right track, too.

That's what this revolution is all about. Wherever leaders are applying its approach, you can find the same daring, the same spirit of engagement, and the same results.

As much as we have accomplished, we cannot and will not rest. Each and every day the pace of change accelerates in our country and the world around us. There are those who want to believe that our world is not changing. There are still others who want change to stop in its tracks. That is not the Democratic way. We will not run from change. We will not pretend change doesn't exist. We will master change. We will harness the dynamic forces driving our world.

Democratic leadership will ensure that we focus on three critical issues.

First, we need to continue our efforts to expand the winner's circle and usher in the areas of our country that have not yet felt the prosperity of the New economy. We need to follow the President's lead and see for ourselves the obstacles these areas face, in the hollows of Appalachia, the migrant worker camps of California, and the rowhouse blocks of East Baltimore.

It cannot be that we have gained this great wealth just so we could afford private security guards and gates to keep those less fortunate than us out of our sight. Now that the stigma of welfare is gone, we can again harness the compassion and ingenuity of our country to bring the dream of progress back to the homes where there are only nightmares. We need to deal with debilitating drug addiction and dangerous housing, violent crime, health care, and make sure every job provides a fair wage. Our progress as a nation depends upon it.

And with the same courage and creativity the Democratic Party has always shown, we need to work together to find solutions. How do we spur investment? How do we develop the skills for the information age? How do we utilize technology? How do we build the infrastructure of progress?

Second, we need to create an education system that truly prepares our country and our citizens for the demands of an information economy. That means bringing a new generation talented, energized teachers into our schools, and making sure all our teachers have the training and tools they need. Providing our students with the revolutionary tools of this new age; creating opportunities for lifelong learning; and raising our expectations, so that a college diploma in the 21st century is as common as a high school diploma is today.

Third, we need to find ways to help parents juggle the demands of work and family. This challenge is multiplying in its complexity and difficulty every day, as more Americans begin caring for their aging parents. In many ways, the strain this puts on people is even greater than that of raising children. We need to work with businesses to create an economy that supports and strengthens families.

These are the issues that matter most to Americans. They are local issues that demand local attention and governance. But they transcend State and even national borders, and they demand national leadership.

We are blessed. We live in an age of discovery. New knowledge is being created, new answers are being found. Old mysteries are solved; old obstacles are conquered. Our nation today has the confidence, the ingenuity, and the resources to tackle any challenge.

We have been offered the opportunity to direct the search for solutions. We have been elected to innovate; to make the tough decisions, to lead our communities and our country into a new age. Our discoveries today will shape our communities and our world for the next century. No generation of leaders in our country's history has been given such a chance.

We can eradicate the opportunity divide running through our country. We can offer everyone the chance to use their talents to pursue their dreams. Most important, we can provide Americans with the time and the means to give of themselves: to their families, communities and country. For the chance to serve is the truest wealth: that is the American Dream.

We will not achieve that dream unless we have a leader who understands the forces at work in our world, and works to extend the blessings of prosperity to every American. That leader is Al Gore. We cannot leave the so-called unprofitable segments of society behind. Democrats stand for opportunity for all; not just for the few.

We will press onward, with a passion to secure justice by erasing the line that divides those with hope from those without. No one will be left behind.

If we stay true to our founding principles, if we meet this new age with hope, purpose, a sense of adventure, and confidence in the American people, no goal will be too lofty. No challenge beyond our reach.

Failure is impossible.

KATHLEEN KENNEDY TOWNSEND

Kathleen Kennedy Townsend, Maryland's first woman Lieutenant Governor, has made it her mission to build safe communities across the state through a comprehensive strategy of effective punishment, policing and prevention. The backbone of the strategy is to create new partnerships between citizens, police, the business and religious communities and public agencies. To develop and oversee the State's anti-crime efforts, Governor Parris Glendening appointed her chair of the state's Cabinet Council on Criminal and Juvenile Justice, which consists of nine cabinet secretaries and the Attorney General.

Through the work of the Cabinet Council and a series of 15 regional crime summits she held across the state Lt. Governor Townsend developed the state's first coordinated and comprehensive anti-crime initiative. Hailed nationally by U.S. Attorney General Reno as the "Townsend Model," the Maryland HotSpot Communities Initiative pulls together previously scattered government agency operations and grant funds to target 36 high-crime and at-risk neighborhoods across Maryland with an unprecedented array of resources for community policing, probation enforcement, nuisance abatement, youth violence and community mobilization.

Mrs. Townsend spearheaded the establishment of Operation Maryland Cease-Fire and the Maryland Community Policing Academy. Cease-Fire is the First State Police unit dedicated to targeting illegal gun traffickers. Since its inception in the summer of 1995, the unit has confiscated hundreds of assault weapons and other illegal firearms and closed a gun store that sold weapons traced to a dozen murders. Also a national first, the Maryland Community Policing Academy trains police and citizens together to build the mutual trust essential for communities to shut down open-air drug markets and make lasting reductions in crime and fear.

Lt. Governor Townsend has strengthened the adult criminal justice system as well. She passed legislation to reduce delays in applying the death penalty and announced a new policy of refusing to grant parole to offenders sentenced to life in prison. The Lt. Governor also is expanding the use of effective immediate punishments such as boot camps, home detention and mandatory drug treatment for nonviolent, drug-addicted offenders.

Along with key legislators, Mrs. Townsend also led the campaign to tighten Maryland's drunk driving laws, working to pass legislation that makes convictions easier to obtain for motorists caught driving with blood alcohol levels of .10 or above.

While tough enforcement and punishment are essential, Mrs. Townsend strongly believes that prevention must be an equal priority. Through the Cabinet Council, she crafted legislation to increase teachers' authority to remove disruptive students from the classroom and establish a statewide student Code of Discipline. Mrs. Townsend created the first Character Education Office in the nation to establish programs that teach honesty, respect, responsibility and other ethical behavior. She also has quadrupled the amount of the state's grant funding targeted to after-school activities for high-risk youth.

As co-chair of the Maryland Family Violence Council, along with the state Attorney General J. Joseph Curran, Mrs. Townsend issued a comprehensive report detailing legal and policy changes needed to protect victims of domestic violence, hold abusers accountable and break the cycle of violence between generations. The Council developed legislation to strengthen civil protection orders and create special probation units to supervise batterers.

Before becoming Lt. Governor, Mr. Townsend served as Deputy Assistant Attorney General in the U.S. Department of Justice. She was responsible for more than $1 billion budget to support local law enforcement and establish community-policing programs across the country.

Committed to providing quality education for all citizens, Mrs. Townsend also has taught at the University of Pennsylvania, the University of Maryland-Baltimore County (UMBC) and at Essex and Dundalk Community Colleges. She was the first Executive Director of the Maryland Student Service Alliance, a public-private partnership she founded with the State Department of Education to inspire young people to serve their communities. Under her leadership, Maryland became the first state in the nation to require all high school students to perform community service. The Alliance also launched Civic Works, an urban service corps that puts young adults to work while teaching critical job skills.

In addition, Mrs. Townsend, a long time advocate for children and families, serves as the Chair of the State's Systems Reform Task Force for Children and Youth. She is a lifelong champion of environmental conservation and a strong proponent of international trade and economic development. The Lt. Governor has been actively involved in all these areas, privately and professionally, publishing articles in The Baltimore Sun, The Washington Post, The New York Times, Ladies Home Journal, The Washington Monthly and in several law reviews. Mrs. Townsend is the founder of the Robert F. Kennedy Human Rights Award and the former chair of the Board of the Robert F. Kennedy Memorial Foundation. She was elected chair of the nation's Democratic Caucus of Lt. Governors. She is the chair of the Oversight Committee of the Peabody Conservatory and founding chair of the Board of Advisors of Maryland's Character Education initiative. She also chairs the External Advisory Board of the Kennedy-

Kreiger Institute's Early Infant Transition Center. Mrs. Townsend serves on Hopkins University Nitze School of Advanced Studies (SAIS); and the Institute of Human Virology of the University of Maryland. Mrs. Townsend serves on the Board of Directors of the National Institute for Women's Policy Research and on the Board of Partners of Radcliffe College.

Born on July 4, 1951, Mrs. Townsend is the eldest child of the late Senator and U.S. Attorney General, Robert F. Kennedy and Mrs. Ethel S. Kennedy. She is cum laude graduate of Harvard University and a graduate of the New Mexico Law School, where she was an editor of the law review. She has received many honorary degrees. Mrs. Townsend lives in Baltimore County with her husband, David, a professor at St. John's College in Annapolis, and two of their four daughters, Kate (14) and Kerry (6). Her oldest daughters, 20-year-old Meaghan and 18-yearold Maeve, are in their junior and freshman years of college.

Kathleen Kennedy Townsend